TAFSIR
Qur'anic Exegesis

TAFSIR

Edited by
Gholamali Haddad Adel
Mohammad Jafar Elmi
Hassan Taromi-Rad

Islamic Book Trust, Kuala Lumpur

Encyclopaedia of the World of Islam

First published 2012
Encyclopaedia of the World of Islam

This edition 2018
Islamic Book Trust
607 Mutiara Majestic, Jalan Othman
46000 Petaling Jaya, Selangor, Malaysia
www.ibtbooks.com

This edition has been published by arrangement with EWI.

Islamic Book Trust is affiliated with The Other Press.

Perpustakaan Negara Malaysia   Cataloguing-in-Publication Data

TAFSIR : QUR'ANIC EXEGESIS: An Entry from Encyclopaedia of the World of Islam / Edited by: Gholamali Haddad Adel, Mohammad Jafar Elmi, Hassan Taromi-Rad.
    Includes index
    Bibliography: page 149
    ISBN 978-967-0526-40-9
    1. Qur'an--Criticism, interpretation.
    2.Qur'an--Hermeneutics. 3. Islam--Encyclopedias.
    I. Haddad Adil, Ghulam Ali. II. Mohammad Jafar Elmi.
    III. Tarimi rad, Hasan.
    297.122601

Printed by
SS Graphic Printers (M) Sdn. Bhd.
Lot 7 & 8, Jalan TIB 3
Taman Industri Bolton
68100 Batu Caves, Selangor

CONTENTS

PREFACE

Today, Islam is recognised as a reality that has left an impact on thoughts, ideas, cultures, and politics in the world. Thus, it has been able to attract the attention of students and researchers over the last few decades. Currently, it can be observed that there is an intensified desire to gain further knowledge concerning the Islamic faith, its foundations, and the ethical values pertaining to the individual and social behaviours of Muslims. Muslim academics and researchers throughout the world have attempted to formulate an Islamic response to the questions that are before mankind. One such response is through writing of different encyclopaedias, of which *The Encyclopaedia of the World of Islam* (*EWI*) is an instance.

The encyclopaedia consists of articles relating to Islamic culture and history; the geography of the Islamic world; and Muslim scholars of various fields of Islamic studies such as Qur'anic and *hadith* studies, Islamic jurisprudence, Qur'anic exegesis, and theology. Other articles are also found in this encyclopaedia relating to the fields of knowledge that have developed during the time of Islamic expansion such as mathematics, astrology, philosophy, and medicine. Additional articles are also available relating to the domains of study essential to the understanding of Islam such as the Arabic language and literature and arts and skills prominent in the Islamic world such as architecture, music, and painting. The range of articles is further exhausted by the fact that this encyclopaedia consists of subjects describing the general life and affairs of Muslim society.

The *EWI* is being published in the Islamic Republic of Iran in Persian. Its Arabic translation has begun and will steadily be brought into print. For English translation it has been decided to translate and publish a series of articles from the *EWI* independently and prior to its ultimate completion so that articles from it could be available to the English language reader.

The current volume is a translation of a series of articles on tafsīr, or Qur'anic exegesis. Beginning with the time of the Prophet Muhammad, this volume traces the development of tafsir step by step through Islamic history. It discusses the primary trends in tafsīr, such as exegesis by narrations, literary exegesis, mystical exegesis, and scientific exegesis. All in all, it provides a comprehensive overview of one of the most fundamental religious sciences in Islamic thought.

In conclusion, the editors would like to acknowledge the contribution of a number of experts, consultants and colleagues without whose efforts this project would not have materialised. First and foremost, we are grateful to the authors for providing solid scholarship on the subject of the ḥawza.

A note of thanks goes to Shuja Ali Mirza who worked diligently to render the entry into English.

We would like to express our gratitude to the editor Mehdi Baghi for his valuable editorial interventions and to Hoda Shafi'i-Shakib for collating the English translation against the original Persian and for checking facts, figures and references. We are indebted to Hamid Tehrani for his advice and consultation throughout this project; and to our industrious colleague Zahra Khaniki who prepared the layout and the index of the present volume.

We greatly appreciate the efforts of Syed Taqi Jaffer Razvi and Ali Aranji for supervising and facilitating the workflow of the present volume.

Gholamali Haddad Adel
Mohammad Jafar Elmi
Hassan Taromi-Rad

TRANSLITERATION SYSTEM

Consonants

ء	'
ب	b
ت	t
ث	th
ج	j
ح	ḥ
خ	kh
د	d
ذ	dh
ر	r
ز	z
س	s
ش	sh
ص	ṣ

ض	ḍ
ط	ṭ
ظ	ẓ
ع	ʿ
غ	gh
ف	f
ق	q
ک	k
ل	l
م	m
ن	n
ه	h
ة	h

Semi-Vowels

و	w, v[1]
ى	y

Short Vowels

َ	a
ُ	u
ِ	i

Long Vowels

ا َ	ā
و ُ	ū
ي ِ	ī

Persian Letters

پ	p
چ	ch
ژ	zh
گ	g

Diphthongs

و َ	aw
ى َ	ay
ي ِّ	iyy
و ُّ	uww

1. *Labio-dental in Persian phonology.*

INTRODUCTION

The term *Tafsīr* is applied to the practice of interpreting and explaining the verses of the Qur'an. This practice was initiated during the Period of Revelation (*'aṣr nuzūl al-waḥy*) by the Holy Prophet (SAW) himself and was continued after his demise. Qur'anic interpretation eventually developed into a discipline, incorporating a multiplicity of approaches and methods. Principles of the discipline have been formulated by experts in addition to the large corpus of Qur'anic exegesis produced in Arabic, Persian, and other languages over fourteen centuries. Such formulations appear both as introductions to works devoted mainly to Qur'anic exegesis or as independent works.

This article examines the subject of Qur'anic exegesis from a historical and a thematic perspective and includes the following topics:

1. general points;
2. interpretation by the Holy Prophet (SAW);

3. exegesis by the the Prophet's Household (AS);
4. exegesis by the Companions (*ṣaḥāba*);
5. exegesis by the Successors (*tābiʿūn*);
6. transmitted (*ma'thūr*) exegesis;
7. literary analysis;
8. jurisprudential exegesis;
9. mystical exegesis;
10. rational exegesis;
11. scientific exegesis;
12. modern approaches to Qur'anic exegesis;
13. hermeneutics in the Islamic world;
14. Orientalists' treatment of Qur'anic exegesis.

1. GENERALITIES

Mihrdād 'Abbāsī

LITERAL MEANING

The literal meaning of the term *tafsīr* is clarification and exposition. There are two options with regard to the derivation of the term. One is that *tafsīr* derives from the root *f-s-r*. Lexicographers offer a number of definitions for the root, including:

1. clarification and explanation (s.v. *f-s-r* in Jawharī, Ibn Fāris, Ibn Manẓūr);

2. uncovering what is obscure (s.v. *f-s-r* in Ibn Manẓūr, Fīrūz Ābādī, Murtaḍā Zabīdī);

3. discovering and expressing the plausible meaning of a word or phrase (s.v. *f-s-r* in Rāghib Iṣfahānī (1332 AHS/1953; Murtaḍā Zabīdī; For more definitions, s.v. *f-s-r* in Farāhīdī, Jawharī, Ibn Fāris, Ibn Manẓūr; Zarkashī, vol. 2, pp. 147-48.).

But all the definitions presented here share the semantic core of explanation and clarification.

Some lexicographers are of the opinion that *tafsīr* and *fasr* denote the same meaning (s.v. *f-s-r* in Farāhīdī, Ibn Durayd, Jawharī, Ibn Fāris, Ibn Manẓūr, Fīrūz *Ābādī*, Murtaḍā Zabīdī). This, however, seems unlikely since, generally speaking, in Arabic morphology, the derived form *tafʿīl* indicates emphasis and amplification (Raḍī al-Dīn Istarābādī, part 1, vol. 1, p. 92). This is confirmed by the definitions listed in Arabic dictionaries (e.g. Ibn Manẓūr, Fīrūz Ābādī, Murtaḍā Zabīdī) for *tafsīr*, in which the latter is defined as conveying a more emphasised nuance of *fasr* (e.g. Fayyūmī and Shartūnī). As such, *tafsīr* denotes revealing the hidden, though plausible, meaning through diligent examination (Ibn ʿĀshūr, vol. 1, p. 10; Maʿrifat, vol. 1, pp. 13-14).

The second opinion concerning the word *tafsīr* is that it derives from the root *s-f-r*, but *f-s-r* is the metathesised form of *s-f-r* (*Muqaddimatān fī ʿUlūm al-Qurʾan*, p. 173; Abū al-Futūḥ Rāzī, vol. 1, pp. 23-24; Zarkashī, vol. 2, p. 147; Suyūṭī, vol. 4, p. 192; Ṭurayḥī, under *f-s-r*). This view is supported by the etymological principle of comprehensive derivation (*ishtiqāq kabīr*), which is prevalent in Arabic (Tahānawī, vol. 1, p. 207; Ṣāliḥ, p. 186). But only those lexicographers who deem "to discover" or "to come to light" as the original meaning of the root *s-f-r* (Ibn Fāris; Ibn Manẓūr, s.v.) can legitimately maintain this view. To corroborate this view, latter lexicographers point out that the two roots (*f-s-r* and *s-f-r*) are similar, not only in form, but also in meaning.

A study of the usages of the two words, however, proves that *f-s-r* commonly refers to non-sensory meaning, whereas *s-f-r* is usually employed in connection with concrete objects (for a better understanding of the semantic distinction between the two roots, s.v. *f-s-r* and *s-f-r* in Ibn Manẓūr, Fayyūmī, Murtaḍā Zabīdī). The renowned lexicographer, Rāghib Iṣfahānī, approves of the distinction (Rāghib, s.v.). Amīn Khūlī also sides with this view, but adds that *tafsīr* could be derived from either of the two, since both imply discovering something and making it manifest (*Dāʾirat al-Maʿārif al-Islāmiyya*, vol. 9, p. 411). It must also be noted that most lexicographers have opted for the first view, overlooking the second view altogether (s.v. *f-s-r* and *s-f-r* in, among others, Farāhīdī, Ibn Durayd, Jawharī, Ibn Fāris, Ibn Manẓūr, and Murtaḍā Zabīdī).

There is the further opinion to the effect that *tafsīr* originated as a Syriac word. In ancient Syriac literature, according to this view, tafsīr denoted exegesis on Holy Scriptures (Jeffery, p. 92; Shahīdī, p. 132).

In the Qurʾan, there is only one occurrence of the word *tafsīr*: "They do not pose to you a conundrum but that We bring you the truth [in reply to them] and the best *tafsīr* [exposition]" (25:33). The verse is in an address to the Holy Prophet concerning objections and doubts cast by the disbelievers of Mecca. God assures the Holy Prophet that He will offer valid replies that will clarify the question in the best manner possible (s.v. the verse in Ṭabarsī and Ṭabāṭabāʾī). Although Qurʾanic exegets disagree as to the meaning of *tafsīr* in this context, most offer such meanings as "explanation," "uncovering," "elaboration," and "signification" (refer to the verse in the following Qurʾanic exegeses: Ṭabarī, Baghawī, Zamakhsharī, Ṭabarsī, Abū al-Futūḥ Rāzī, and Ālūsī; for further details, see Bābāʾī et al., pp. 10-12).

TECHNICAL DEFINITION

In its broad sense, the term *tafsīr* is applied to any exegesis or exposition of a scientific, literary, or philosophical work (*"Tafsīr," Encyclopedia of Islam*, 1st ed.). Exegeses on the works of Aristotle and Euclid and those on collections of poetry are referred to as tafsīr (e.g. Qifṭī, pp. 97, 99-100, 275, 288; Ḥājī Khalīfa, vol. 1, col. 462; Āqā Buzurg Ṭihrānī, vol. 4, pp. 346-351). But it is used in a yet different context to indicate a literary tool consisting of a poet's clarifying what he had previously mentioned briefly and ambiguously (Ibn Rashīq, vol. 2, p. 35; Yaḥyā ibn Ḥamza Yamanī, vol. 3, pp. 114-15; Ibn 'Āshūr, vol. 1, p. 10; *Encyclopedia of Religion*, vol. 14, p. 236). But due to its frequent use in connection with the science of Qur'anic exegesis, the term *tafsīr*, when used unmodified, is commonly understood among Islamic scholars and Muslims in general to refer to the particular Qur'anic discipline.

Early Qur'anic exegets were of different opinions on whether or not to characterise Qur'anic exegesis as a distinct discipline. Ibn 'Āshūr holds (vol. 1, p. 12) that such a characterisation would be inaccurate as Qur'anic exegesis was practised well before any discrete Islamic discipline solidified. In time and through discussion and debate, scholars of Islam developed certain principles upon which Qur'anic exegesis should be based. In this way they acquired a body of knowledge related in the main to an understanding of the Qur'an, which they defined as the science of Qur'anic exegesis (Ibn 'Āshūr, vol. 1, p. 13).

This difference in viewing Qur'anic exegesis as a distinct discipline inevitably led to a discrepancy in defining it. Amīn Khūlī (*Dā'irat al-Ma'ārif al-Islāmiyya*, vol. 9, p. 411) speaks of two views on the definition of the discipline of Qur'anic exegesis. According to one view posited by early scholars, Qur'anic exegesis does not fit into the category of rational sciences, for it does not involve a definite set of principles. As a result, those subscribing to this view are not concerned with putting forth a particular subject matter or delimiting the questions of this practice. They simply state that the practice of Qur'anic exegesis is the attempt to clarify the Word of God or, in other words, to shed light on the phraseology and content of the verses of the Qur'an.

According to the second view, the exercise of Qur'anic exegesis is a distinct discipline. Those in favour of this position take pains to offer a clear definition for Qur'anic exegesis. The problem with this view is that the consequent definitions are flawed by failing to duly distinguish Qur'anic exegesis from other disciplines or for including in the definition studies that serve as prerequisites for understanding the Qur'an (a number of these definitions appear below).

Amīn Khūlī prefers the first view since it abstains from any unwanted prolixity (*Dā'irat al-Ma'ārif al-Islāmiyya*, vol. 9, p. 411). Dhahabī (vol. 1, pp. 14-16) expresses the same idea verbatim, only adding that the knowledge of Qur'anic recitation (*qirā'a*) and orthography (*rasm al-khaṭṭ*) is included in the science of Qur'anic exegesis. His reason for this inclusion is that the meaning of a verse may differ owing to divergent views in these two fields (Dhahabī vol. 1, p. 15). According to Dhahabī, although proponents of the second view have offered various definitions for *tafsīr*, which appear to differ, the definitions all come down to the same concept (see below).

Most exegets, however, have avoided the trouble of defining this discipline, most likely because they found it sufficiently evident (Ṭabarī, Zamakhsharī, Fakhr Rāzī, Ibn 'Aṭiyya, Tha'ālibī, Ibn Jawzī, and Bayḍāwī, for instance, provide no definition of tafsīr in the introductions to their Qur'anic exegeses). Such definitions appear commonly in sources on Qur'anic studies and, occasionally, in introductions to Qur'anic exegeses.

Some Islamic scholars have extended the definition of Qur'anic exegesis to encompass all the Qur'anic and religious studies. Ṭūsī (vol. 1, p. 2), for instance, considers anything related to the clarification and understanding of the meaning of the Qur'an—e.g., the study of recitation (*qirā'a*), Arabic eloquence and syntax, the study of the equivocal verses, Islamic apologetics—as falling within the scope of the discipline of Qur'anic exegesis.

In one of the two definitions presented for the science of Qur'anic exegesis, Zarkashī (vol. 2, p. 148) includes the following topics: occasion of revelation, place of revelation, i.e., whether a verse is Makkī or Madanī, the abrogated and abrogating verses, general and particular verses, absolute and qualified verses, the permissible and impermissible, and Divine precepts (for his other definition, see vol. 1, p. 13; see also Suyūṭī, vol. 4, p. 194). According to Abū Ḥayyān Gharnāṭī (vol. 1, pp. 13-14), the science of Qur'anic exegesis comprises the study of recitation, punctuation, vocalisation, the analysis of the meaning of words used in the Qur'an and their morphology, and other such related topics. As such, Abū Ḥayyān's definition recognises, on the one hand, the knowledge of Qur'anic recitation, orthography, Arabic lexicon, morphology, syntax, and eloquence, which constitute the fundamental elements for understanding the Qur'an, and, on the other hand, it includes the study of the abrogated and abrogating verses and the occasions of revelation.

In yet another definition, Qur'anic exegesis is identified as the task of discovering the various aspects of the words in the Qur'an, as the sacred scripture of Islam and as signifying what is intended by God, to the extent possible for human understanding (this signification could be definite or contingent; Ḥājī Khalīfa, vol. 1, col. 428; Ṣiddīq Ḥasan Khān, vol. 1, p. 11; Ṭabarsī, vol. 1 and the Introduction by Aḥmad Riḍa p. 60; all the above relate this definition from Muḥammad ibn Ḥamza Fanārī, d. 834/1430-31). Many recent Islamic scholars prefer the latter definition to include the qualification "to the extent possible for human understanding"; thus Zurqānī (vol. 2, p. 3) and Dhahabī (vol. 1, p. 16) both include this qualification in their definitions (Ḥājī Khalīfa, vol. 1, col. 427; Ṭabarsī, vol. 1, p. 60; Ṣaghīr, p. 19).

Despite the difference in expression in the numerous definitions offered for the science of Qur'anic exegesis (for other definitions, see *'Ulūm al-Qur'an 'ind al-Mufassirīn*, vol. 3, pp. 169-186; and Bābā'ī et. al., pp. 12-23), they all agree in that this discipline treats of the meaning and intention of Qur'anic words and phrases of the Qur'an. In this light, there is a noticeable connection between the literal and technical meanings of tafsīr (Ibn 'Āshūr, vol. 1, pp. 11-12; Ṣaghīr, p. 19). It can be concluded then that Qur'anic exegesis or tafsīr is the endeavour to understand the meaning and intention of Qur'anic words and phrases. For this reason, some scholars have argued that Qur'anic exegesis may be exercised when there is ambiguity in Qur'anic words and phrases whereby the exeget strives to remove ambiguities with diligent examination (Ḥakīm, pp. 68-9; Maʿrifat, vol. 1, p. 14).

TAFSĪR AND *TA'WĪL*

Due to the disagreement among Qur'anic exegets and scholars of Qur'anic studies on the meaning of *ta'wīl*, different views have been offered as to its relation to *tafsīr* (for further details, see *'Ulūm al-Qur'an 'ind al-Mufassirīn*, vol. 3, pp. 203-216; Ṣaghīr, pp. 20-23). Some scholars, in fact, have identified the two as synonymous. This view, attributed to such eminent early literary figures as Abū 'Ubayd Qāsim ibn Sallām (d. 224/838-39) and Abū al-'Abbās Mubarrad (d. 286/899; Suyūṭī, vol. 4, p. 192; Ṭabarsī, vol. 1, p. 80), is considered the prevalent view among early exegets (Ibn Jawzī, vol. 1, p. 4). However, there were early scholars, e.g. Ḥabīb Nayshābūrī (d. 245/859-60), who rejected this view (Zarkashī, vol. 2, p. 152; Suyūṭī, vol. 4, p. 192).

Apparently the term *ta'wīl* was employed in scholarly circles in Mecca in the latter part of the third/ninth century to denote Qur'anic exegesis. Nearly a century later, it was replaced by the term *Tafsīr* (*Encyclopedia of Religion*, vol. 14, p. 236). A comparison between the two terms does likewise appear in the works of such early luminaries as Muqātil ibn Sulaymān (d. 150/767-68; vol. 1, pp. 25-27), Ṭabarī (d. 310/922-23; vol. 1, p. 26), and Māturīdī (d. 333/944-45, also see Suyūṭī). Yet when it came to giving a name to their Qur'anic exegeses, both Ṭabarī and Māturīdī chose *ta'wīl* as the term to denote exposition of the Qur'an, as is evident in the titles of their exegeses: *Jāmi' al-Bayān 'an Ta'wīl Āyī al-Qur'an* and *Ta'wīlāt Ahl al-Sunna*, respectively. (For more detail, see *Encyclopedia of Religion*, vol. 14, p. 236; 'Iwaḍīn's introduction to Māturīdī, vol. 1, pp. 23-5)

According to Rāghib (1405/1983, p. 47), *tafsīr* is mainly employed in connection with individual words, whereas *ta'wīl* is predominantly applied to the meaning and the phrases. He also adds another distinction: that the use of *ta'wīl* is restricted to sacred scriptures, whereas *tafsīr* is used to describe exegeses on ordinary books as well (Suyūṭī, vol. 4, p. 192).

Most of the later Qur'anic scholars, however, have maintained that *ta'wīl* is fundamentally distinct in meaning from *tafsīr*. According to this view, *tafsīr* clarifies the meaning of the constituent words and of the sentences; ta'wīl, on the other hand, is concerned with, according to one view, judging among the different possible meanings of a verse or, according to a rival view, discovering the esoteric meaning of the verses. Ṭabarsī (ibid.), for instance, though considering both terms as relating to the meaning of Qur'anic verses, deems *tafsīr* as the practice of discovering the meaning of the difficult phrases and *ta'wīl* as that of determining the most likely meaning where a verse allows of more than one interpretation (Jurjānī, pp. 72-87). Abū Ṭālib Taghlibī (Suyūṭī, vol. 4, p. 193; Ḥājī Khalīfa, vol. 1, col. 334) describes *tafsīr* as the discipline responsible for uncovering the exoteric meaning and *ta'wīl* as that dealing with the esoteric dimension ('Askarī, p. 131).

Māturīdī views *tafsīr* as the endeavour to ascertain the meaning of Qur'anic words as intended by God and offering evidence to this end. He defines *ta'wīl* as determining the most likely meaning (without necessarily having to establish this with certainty) where there are more than one possibility but without the requirement of substantiating it with evidence (apud Suyūṭī, vol. 4, p. 192). A number of recent Qur'anic scholars have opted for this view, distinguishing the two terms as: "*Tafsīr*'s signification is definitive, but *ta'wīl*'s is conjectural" (Ahl, p. 58; Ṣaghīr, p. 23).

Another view is that *tafsīr* is concerned with the meaning of Qur'anic verses where they are sufficiently clear or where they have been interpreted by the Prophet's actionsand words (*sunna*). Consequently, there is no room for speculation and extrapolation in *tafsīr*. Whereas, *ta'wīl*, is the acquisition of learned scholars who have a deep understanding of the Divine and God's Word (Zarkashī, vol. 2, p. 150; Suyūṭī, vol. 4, p. 194). Zarkashī (vol. 2, p. 172) finds this distinction plausible and is of the opinion that the difference between *tafsīr* and *ta'wīl* goes back to that between transmitted doctrine (*naql*) and discursive reasoning (*'aql*). In other words, *tafsīr* is confined to narrating the interpretations offered by religious authorities, whereas *ta'wīl* derives from extrapolation and *rational* reasoning (Zarkashī, vol. 2, p. 172; Suyūṭī, vol. 4, pp. 193-94 according to Abū Naṣr Qushayrī, d. 514/1120; Khāzin, vol. 1, p. 15).

Ālūsī, while Refuting his colleagues, claims (vol. 1, p. 5) that none of the explanations offered for the difference between the two terms are correct in the context of contemporary Qur'anic sciences. He argues that in contemporary usage, *ta'wīl* refers to the spiritual and esoteric meaning that God reveals to the heart of the mystic through Divine inspiration, and *tafsīr* indicates the exposition of the exoteric meaning.

Ibn Taymiyya (vol. 2, p. 103, vol. 7, p. 444) also offers his own definition of the two terms. He explains that in the language of the Qur'an, *ta'wīl* is the existential and objective truth of God's Word, just as *tafsīr* is the conceptual and subjective truth. Apparently this opinion is borrowed from Rāghib Iṣfahānī ("*Ta'wīl*," *Dā'irat al-Ma'ārif al-Islāmiyya*, vol. 9, p. 411).

SIGNIFICANCE AND NECESSITY OF QUR'ANIC EXEGESIS

The Qur'an was revealed among the Arabs and as such is in Arabic. But Arabs were not all proficient in their command of the Arabic language. Thus, the Holy Prophet, from the very start, embarked on explaining and clarifying the difficult words and ambiguous phrases and pointing out abrogating and abrogated verses (Ibn Khaldūn, vol. 1, "Introduction," p. 554). Zarkashī (vol. 1 pp. 14-15) believes that during the Period of Revelation, Arabs acquired knowledge of the subtleties of the Qur'an and its esoteric meaning from the Holy Prophet. The great part of this knowledge of *tafsīr* and *ta'wīl*, however, was not passed down to Muslims of later generations.

This gap rendered Muslims seriously in need of engaging in Qur'anic exegesis. This need is especially accentuated once we realise that Qur'anic exegesis is concerned not only with the theoretical aspect of Qur'anic knowledge but also with the practical aspect, consisting of reconciling the conduct of Muslims and the circumstances of the times with the Qur'an (*Encyclopedia of Religion*, vol. 14, p. 237). Muslims have always sought to duly understand the meaning and essence of God's Word in order to practice its precepts and injunctions (*The Oxford Encyclopedia of the Modern Islamic World*, vol. 4, p. 170). It is in this way that Muslims' need for the science of Qur'anic exegesis is timeless.

Although the Qur'an, on a variety of occasions, describes itself as "clear" and "clarifying" (e.g. 3:138; 5:15; 16:89), there are certain qualities in it that lead to ambiguity and difficulty in understanding some of its verses (Ma'rifat, vol. 1, p. 14). The most important of such qualities relate to the Qur'anic method of expression, which can be summarised into three general distinctions. First, the Qur'an conveys an extensive body of profound knowledge through an inevitably limited number of words, which unavoidably entails ambiguity. This is evident in the verses of the Qur'an that deal with practical injunctions, to whose exposition the Holy Prophet had been entrusted (16:44; Kulaynī, vol. 1, pp. 286-87). Second, a number of Qur'anic verses speak of supernatural truths concerning the World of Unseen. Comprehending such truths was obviously impossible or, at best, difficult for a large number of people at the time of revelation, and this applies to all times. Third, the verses of the Qur'an do not follow a thematic pattern. Thus there are many examples where one chapter (*sūra*) or verse (*āya*) contains numerous topics (Qummī, vol. 1, p. 19; ʿAyyāshī, vol. 1, p. 11). The problems caused by these qualities are further exacerbated due to the obscurity of certain Qurʾanic terms and the length of time that separates us from the Period of Revelation (Rāghib Iṣfahānī, 1405/1983, pp. 47-48). The combination of these elements makes the science of Qurʾanic exegesis of critical importance (for further details, see Maʿrifat, vol. 1, pp. 14-16; and Bābāʾī et. al., pp. 36-40).

Another point is that the teachings of the Qurʾan are multivalent, i.e., possessing multiple levels of meaning. According to a hadith (Ḥuwayzī, vol. 1, p. 313; Qummī Mashhadī, vol. 3, p. 32), Qurʾanic teachings are defined in three levels when understanding it in relation to its revelation; mysteries, smooth flow, and intricate nature. The first and easiest level is comprehensible for common people without the need for interpretation or exposition. The second level is that which lies beyond the ken of ordinary people and can be acquired only through exposition and examination. We can partake of this level proportionate to the extent of our knowledge and capability. The third level is exclusive to God's prophets and the "firmly established in knowledge" (cf. Ṭabarī, vol. 1, p. 26; Ṭabarsī, vol. 1, p. 81).

It is to acquire the second level of understanding, which encompasses a vast body of knowledge, that Qurʾanic exegesis is instrumental, and it is to fulfill this need that this discipline has been practised throughout the history of Islamic scholarship. The Qurʾan also addresses this need, exhorting the believers to contemplate its content (4:82; 38:29; 47:24) for the purpose of realising this second level of Qurʾanic understanding, which necessarily involves an examination of the words and phrases of the Qurʾan.

Although Muslims' own needs are sufficiently manifest to make the science of Qurʾanic exegesis indispensible, there are sayings by eminent personages that confirm this necessity. There are several examples. Pertaining to the verse "and he to

whom is granted wisdom is indeed granted Abundant good"
(2:269), many Qur'anic exegets have interpreted "wisdom" as the
knowledge of Qur'anic exegesis (Ṭabarī, vol. 3, p. 60; Ṭabarsī,
vol. 2, p. 659; Quṭrubī, vol. 3, p. 330; Ibn Kathīr, vol. 1, p. 504).
In explaining a hadith related from the Holy Prophet—*i'rabū
al-Qur'an wa iltamisū gharā'ibahū*—(Ḥakim Nayshābūrī, vol. 2,
p. 439; Ṭabarsī, vol. 1, p. 81) Suyūṭī (vol. 4 p. 198) is convinced
that *i'rabū al-Qur'an* signifies Qur'anic exegesis and adds that
scholars are unanimous in acknowledging Qur'anic exegesis as
the noblest of Islamic sciences and as a collective duty (*wājib al-
kifā'ī*; Suyūṭī, vol. 4, p. 199).

There are also many sayings in this relation attributed
to the Companions (*ṣaḥāba*) and the Successors (*tābi'ūn*).
Reprimanding a person for reciting the Qur'an without
attention to its interpretation, Ibn 'Abbās likened him to an
illiterate, hastily and unmindfully mouthing lines of poetry
(apud Tha'ālibī, vol. 1, p. 28). Mujāhid considers the person
with the greatest knowledge of the Qur'an as the most favoured
servant in the sight of God (apud Quṭrubī, vol. 1, p. 26). There
is also a claim to the effect about numerous hadiths related in
the corpus of Islamic tradition concerning the rewards that
Qur'anic recitation earns for the believer (e.g. Tirmidhī, vol. 5,
p. 5-27; and Ibn Bābiwayh, pp. 104-129) intends for a recitation
to be accompanied by thought and contemplation (Ṣiddīq
Ḥasan Khān, vol. 1, p. 21).

Rāghib Iṣfahānī (1405/1983, p. 91) believes that Qur'anic
exegesis is the highest knowledge one may learn, for the nobility
of a knowledge is determined by the value of its subject — and
in the case of Qur'anic exegesis, this is the Word of God — or by
the value of its purpose, which in the case of the Qur'an, is true
felicity by understanding God's message — or by the degree of
one's need for it, which is most crucial in the case of the exegesis
as the acquisition of any human perfection rests on it. As such,
the science of Qur'anic exegesis is the noblest discipline in every
respect (Bayḍāwī, vol. 1, p. 4; Ālūsī, vol. 1, p. 5).

REQUIREMENTS OF THE PRACTICE OF QUR'ANIC EXEGESIS

The divergent methods and approaches taken by Qur'anic exegets throughout the long history of this discipline have led to numerous disagreements and, occasionally, inaccuracies in expressing the meaning of the verses of the Qur'an. This demonstrates that in the discipline of Qur'anic exegesis, as in any discipline, there is a need for certain principles. In addition to reducing disagreements and errors to a minimum, these also serve as a means for assessing Qur'anic exegeses and preventing extrapolation and erroneous readings. Thus, the requirements of *tafsīr* are factors that, if disregarded, would lead to errors in interpretation and to loss of credibility. Interpretation by personal opinion (*tafsīr bi-'l-ra'y*) is, for instance, viewed as such a violation (see below). The most critical requirements as viewed by experts in the field are firstly, acquiring the preliminary sciences needed for a correct understanding of the Qur'an secondly, drawing on credible sources of Qur'anic exegesis and thirdly, observing the rules of exegesis (Rāghib Iṣfahānī, 1405/1983, pp. 96-7; Suyūṭī, vol. 4, p. 216; Zurqānī, vol. 2, p. 51; Dhahabī, vol. 1, pp. 266, 273, 275).

Numerous sciences have been postulated as the requisite for a correct understanding of the Qur'an — and there is disagreement on the number of these sciences (Kāfiyajī, p. 10) — but the most important unanimously agreed upon are the following: 1. the literary sciences (i.e., Arabic philology, morphology, syntax, and rhetoric), 2. the Qur'anic sciences, i.e., the knowledge of Qur'anic recitation, the abrogated and abrogating verses, and the occasions of revelation, 3. hadith sciences, including contextual study of hadith (*dirāya*) and transmission authorities (*rijāl*), 4. principles of jurisprudence (*uṣūl al-fiqh*), 5. Jurisprudence (*fiqh*), 6. theology (*kalām*), 7. Divine inspiration (*mawhibah*; Rāghib Iṣfahānī, 1405/1983, pp. 94-6; Kāfiyajī, pp. 10-12; Suyūṭī, vol. 4, pp. 213-215).

A good grasp of philology enables the exeget to know the true and metaphorical meanings of the words of the Qur'an. Morphology and syntax are necessary to understand the individual structure of the words and that of the sentence as a combination of a number of words. And by comprehending eloquence of Arabic, the exeget can realise how the Qur'an addresses its audience by employing such devices as simile and metaphor. By knowing the Qur'anic sciences, the exeget can furthermore distinguish the correct form of the words of the Qur'an, the order of revelation of the verses, and the occasions of revelation. Because of the inseparable connection between the Qur'an and hadith, the exeget must be also well acquainted with the phraseology of hadiths and their transmitters. The science of *uṣūl al-fiqh* equips the exeget with the principles he needs to determine what the verses denote and how the connotation is binding. The necessity of being familiar with jurisprudence and theology stems from the fact that the Qur'an contains verses pertaining to the like issues.

From among the sciences essential for correct interpretation, Divine inspiration is different from the rest in its method of acquisition. The exeget obtains this knowledge by sincerely observing what he believes in. God bestows this knowledge on anyone who truly acts according to what he knows (Rāghib Iṣfahānī, 1405/1983, pp. 95-6; Kāfiyajī, p. 12). There are many verses (e.g. 2:282; 8:29; 29:69) and hadiths (Quṭrubī, vol. 13, p. 364; Ibn Kathīr, vol. 4, p. 879; Fayḍ Kāshānī, vol. 1, p. 468; Majlisī, vol. 40, p. 128) suggesting the more pure one's heart is, the better is one's understanding of the Qur'an. Ālūsī, however, challenges this view (vol. 1, p. 6), refuting the necessity of this science and its effect on understanding the Qur'an but rather relevant to the rational reasoning of *ta'wīl* (for further details on the function of these sciences in Qur'anic exegesis, see Zamakhsharī, vol. 1, p. *ṣād nūn*; Ibn Juzayy, vol. 1, pp. 6-8; Abū Ḥayyān Gharnāṭī, vol. 1, pp. 5-7; Suyūṭī, vol. 4, pp. 213-15; Ālūsī, vol. 1, pp. 5-6; Ibn 'Āshūr, vol. 1, pp. 18-27).

Rashīd Riḍā (vol. 1, pp. 21-24) deals with the sciences necessary for Qur'anic exegesis in an entirely different approach. He holds that knowing these sciences is needed only for the highest levels of understanding the Qur'an.

Another aspect of Qu'ranic exegesis which requires attention is making use of credible sources. One kind consists of the transmitted (*naqlī*) material: the Qur'an, the hadiths narrated from the Holy Prophet and the Prophet's Household, and the sayings and opinions attributed to the Companions and Successors. With regard to the Qur'an, it must be pointed out that its verses interpret one another. This method of studying the Qur'an by examining the internal relation among its verses is supported by reason and confirmed by the Prophet's Household and their disciples (Ṭabāṭabā'ī, vol. 1, p. 12; 'Ayyāshī, vol. 1, pp. 55, 202; Ṭabarsī, vol. 7, p. 93). The hadiths narrated from the Holy Prophet are also credible sources as he is introduced by God as the expositor and teacher of the Qur'an (16:44). According to the Shī'a doctrine, the hadiths of the Prophet's Household have a parity with those of the Holy Prophet (Ṭūsī, vol. 1, p. 4).

The sayings of the eminent Companions are also a source for Qur'anic exegesis as they were the Holy Prophet's (SAW) contemporaries and witnessed the Period of Revelation (Suyūṭī, vol. 4, pp. 208-09). The Successors' sayings can also help in the process of Qur'anic exegesis (ibid.). Of course, there is a difference of opinion among scholars as to the credibility of the Companions' and Successors' sayings (Ma'rifat, vol. 1, pp. 307, 431-32).

The second category of sources pertains to language. These sources are important in that they are necessary for determining the meanings and usages of the Qur'anic words at the time of revelation. These meanings and usages may be inferred from contextual indications in the Qur'an, the corpus of hadith, the sayings of the Companions, or the body of Arabic literature pre-dating the revelation of the Qur'an, for example the pre-Islamic poetry. Dictionaries, especially those closer to the Period of Revelation, may also be of help in this regard (Abū Ḥayyān

Gharnāṭī, vol. 1, p. 6; and Zarkashī, vol. 2, pp. 160, 165).

The third category of Qur'anic resources is the exeget's expertise in interpretive judgment (Zarkashī, vol. 2, p. 161), also referred to as the source of discernment (Ṣaghīr, p. 70; Bābā'ī et. al, p. 311).

Observing the rules of exegesis is also necessary for arriving at the correct interpretation (Ṭayyār, p. 87). The relation of these rules to Qur'anic exegesis is that of principles of jurisprudence to jurisprudence or that of syntax to Arabic language (Ṣabbāgh, p. 10). A large number of these rules are scattered throughout Qur'anic exegeses, and sources on principles of jurisprudence, rhetoric, and lexicon. These have not as yet been systematically formulated. Ṭayyār (pp. 87, 94), however, distinguishes two categories of such rules: general rules and preferential rules. He defines general rules as those that must be heeded in expressing the meaning of a verse, and preferential rules as those necessary for preferring one reading over the others when there are multiple possibilities (for further details on the rules of exegesis, see Ṭayyār, pp. 87-121; Rūmī, pp. 136-143). Engaging in Qur'anic exegesis without observing these rules is a flagrant instance of interpretation by personal opinion (Kāfiyajī, p. 12; Suyūṭī, vol. 4, p. 216; Dhahabī, vol. 1, p. 266; Shahīdī, p. 139).

INTERPRETATION BY PERSONAL OPINION

The discussion on interpretation by personal opinion (*tafsīr bi-'l-ra'y*) is raised by one fundamental question: in the absence of explanation from the Infallibles, the Companions, the Successors, and the consensus of opinion among the exegets of the past, are exegets justified in offering their personal view of the meaning of a Qur'anic verse? On this question, there is disagreement among scholars going back to the early periods of Islamic scholarship. These include two diametrically opposed viewpoints.

Some have taken a firm stance against the interpretation

of the Qur'an based on one's personal understanding, even considering this as blasphemy by the most learned scholars, unless a saying from the Holy Prophet, the Companions, or the Successors is cited in support of the position (Rāghib Iṣfahānī, 1405/1983, p. 93). To substantiate their view, these scholars cite hadiths that condemn interpretation by personal opinion (see below) and in addition posit a number of rationales, including: 1. Interpretation by personal opinion involves attributing something unrightfully to God, which is considered a forbidden act in the Qur'an (7:33) 2. Some of the Companions and Successors were cautious not to engage in Qur'anic exegesis; they were obdurate in avoiding Qur'anic exegesis (for more detail in this regard and the refutation of these arguments, see Zurqānī, vol. 2, pp. 54-57; Dhahabī, vol. 1, pp. 257-262).

But there are also scholars who, under certain conditions, allow interpreting the Qur'an based on one's personal understanding. These too produce their arguments. They argue that in numerous verses, the Qur'an encourages believers to reflect on the Qur'an (4:82; 47:24), and this shows that reason and personal understanding are valid means for interpreting the Qur'an. And the fact that the Companions differed on this question is evidence that they too acknowledged the reliability of personal judgment in interpreting the Qur'an (for further details, see Zurqānī, vol. 2, pp. 57-59; Dhahabī, vol. 1, pp. 262-64).

On examination, it seems clear that the source of the disagreement lies in the body of hadiths, recorded in the Shī'a as well as the Sunnī corpora, condemning interpretation by personal opinion (Ṭabarī, vol. 1, p. 27; 'Ayyāshī, vol. 1, pp. 17-8). Of these hadiths, two have been cited more than the rest. One of the two is related from Ibn 'Abbās (Tirmidhī, vol. 5, p. 66, no. 2951; Nisā'ī, vol. 5, p. 31, no. 8085) and the other from Jundub (Abū Dāwūd, vol. 3, p. 320, no. 3652; Tirmidhī, vol. 5, p. 66, no. 2952; and Nisā'ī, vol. 5, p. 31, no. 8086). According to the former, Hell is the abode of those who interpret the Qur'an based on their personal understanding and make repetitive assertions about the Qur'an in accordance with their own opinions. The latter states that interpreting the Qur'an based on one's personal understanding is wrong, even though one's understanding be correct. Some scholars have tried to discredit these hadiths as apocryphal (Tirmidhī, vol. 5, p. 66, no. 2952; Ālūsī, vol. 1, p. 6; Bābā'ī et. al., p. 56), but the main debate has centered on what these hadiths actually mean and what the Holy Prophet intended by interpretation by means of personal opinion.

Ibn Anbārī (d. 328/939-40) is of the opinion that the hadith related from Ibn 'Abbās concerns one who intentionally puts forth a false interpretation. He understands Jundub's hadith as condemning the opinion based on personal judgment, and thus one who interprets the Qur'an in such a way that is not derived from the early authorities, is guilty of impiety, even if the opinion is in itself correct (Quṭrubī, vol. 1, p. 32).

Ibn 'Aṭiyya (vol. 1, p. 17-18) maintains that these hadiths denounce interpretation based on personal opinion that does not take into account the views of the early authorities and does not satisfy the rules of the sciences (see above) necessary for a correct understanding of the Qur'an—such as Arabic syntax and principles of jurisprudence. Thus, in his opinion, scholars versed in Arabic lexicography and syntax or in jurisprudence, who engage in Qur'anic exegesis observing the rules of their respective sciences, are not guilty of interpretation by personal opinion.

Abū Ḥayyān Gharnāṭī (vol. 1, p. 13) states that these hadiths do not apply to the scholars whose interpretation is the result of considering the Qur'an in line with the criteria established in the requisite sciences. Shāṭibī (vol. 3, p. 255) regards the condemnation voiced in these hadiths as addressing the interpretation that disregards the principles of Arabic language and contradicts religious precepts.

In the introduction to his Qur'anic exegesis, Ṭabarsī (vol. 1, pp. 80-81) also takes up this question. He first affirms that interpreting the Qur'an without recourse to authentic and clear hadiths narrated from the Infallibles is impermissible. He then enters the discussion by saying that some of the Successors denounced interpretation by personal opinion (Ṭūsī, vol. 1, p. 4) and, citing evidence from the Qur'an and hadiths, explains Jundub's hadith as intending personal interpretation disregarding contextual and extra-contextual modifiers (Ālūsī, vol. 1, p. 6).

Analysing the two hadiths, 'Allāma Ṭabāṭabā'ī infers that the qualification of opinion (*ra'y*) in both hadiths by the pronoun ("He who interprets the Qur'an according to *his* opinion...") demonstrates that what is intended is not the condemnation of employing thought as such in the interpretation the Qur'an but doing so without consulting the authoritative sources. He views the condemnation in these hadiths as a methodological issue, i.e., it would be wrong to assume that we could interpret the Qur'an as we commonly interpret one another's words. Clearly this does not mean that God's word differs from human communication in its usage of words, sentences, and rhetorical devices. The difference lies in the meanings and tangible instances to which the Qur'an intends. In other words, due to the Qur'anic distinctive mode of expression and interconnectivity of its verses, it would be mistaken to try to interpret one verse without taking into account the related Qur'anic verses (for further details, see Ṭabāṭabā'ī, vol. 3, pp. 76-7; Ma'rifat, vol. 1, pp. 74-5).

Quṭrubī (vol. 1, pp. 33-4) enumerates various views on this question and concludes that the instances of interpretation by personal opinion considered by the exegets may be reduced to two general cases. One case consists of interpreting the Qur'an in accordance with one's personal inclinations and opinions. This may be carried out advertently for the purpose of winning a debate or in good faith for promoting piety in society. It may also be done inadvertently. But in any case, the interpretation is arbitrary. The second case is that the exeget assumes that knowing Arabic is sufficient for understanding the Qur'an and thus does not take it upon himself to study the transmitted material dealing with the meaning of the Qur'an or examine its obscure vocabulary (Fayḍ Kāshānī, vol. 1, pp. 36-8). Quṭrubī believes (vol. 1, p. 34) that the exeget must have recourse to transmitted material in understanding the Qur'an, for this, on the one hand, prevents many an error and, on the other hand, expands his scope of understanding.

In this light, exegeses based on transmitted material and those based on individual judgment (*ijtihād*)— termed by a number of scholars as commendable, praiseworthy, and/or permissible interpretation by personal opinion (Zurqānī, vol. 2, pp. 33, 50; Dhahabī, vol. 1, pp. 273-284)—are complementary; neither is complete without the other. On the one hand, learning the sciences necessary for Qur'anic exegesis is possible only through studying transmitted material, while on the other hand, restricting oneself to transmitted material may prevent a thorough understanding of the Qur'an (Abū Ḥujr, p. 59). It should also be borne in mind that when we interpret the Qur'an based on our understanding, even if all the rules and criteria are observed, our appreciation would not be valid should there be a transmitted interpretation contradicting it. If, however, they do not contradict, they would only serve to corroborate each other (Ṣāliḥ, 1363 AHS/1983, p. 293).

HISTORICAL DEVELOPMENT OF THE SCIENCE OF QUR'ANIC EXEGESIS AND ITS VARIOUS TYPES

It was the Holy Prophet who first initiated Qur'anic exegesis. As Messenger of God, it was his responsibility to answer all questions relating to the Qur'an: to clarify its ambiguities and difficulties. After his death, Qur'anic exegesis continued within two traditions: the tradition of the Prophet's Household and that of the Companions.

According to Shī'a belief, the hadith of the two weighty things (*thiqalayn*) expressly affirms the authority of the Household of the Holy Prophet in questions of religion, including the interpretation of the Qur'an. Based on this and other evidence, the interpretation provided by the Prophet's Household, which is the source of Shī'a transmitted interpretation, is authoritative. Other types of Qur'anic exegesis within the Shī'a school also stem from this tradition.

The rival tradition, however, was established by the majority of the Companions, who, instead of accepting 'Alī's succession, opted for the caliphate. Owing to their association with the Holy Prophet and their presence in the environment of revelation, Muslims saw them as authorities for answering questions on the Qur'an. In addition to narrating the hadiths of the Holy Prophet, the Companions also imparted their own opinions.

With the passage of time and the expansion of the Islamic empire, the Companions travelled to different parts, each founding his own school and training students. Thus, every region had its distinct school of Qur'anic exegesis. These schools flourished under the Successors, and thus the interpretation by the Successors came about. The most prominent schools of Qur'anic exegesis under the tutelage of the Companions were 1. the school of Ibn 'Abbās in Mecca, 2. that of Ubayy ibn Ka'b in Medina, 3. that of Ibn Mas'ūd in Iraq (Dhahabī, vol. 1, pp. 106-07, 118, 121). In these schools such Successors as Mujāhid, 'Ikrima, Ḥasan Baṣrī, Abū al-'Ālīya, and Qatāda studied and rose to prominence.

Up to this stage, Qur'anic exegesis was mainly an oral tradition comprised in large part of hadiths from the Holy Prophet. As such, the first stage in the development of the science of Qur'anic exegesis is characterised as the stage of the transmission of Prophetic hadiths (*riwāya*; Dhahabī, vol. 1, p. 145; Ṣaghīr, p. 138). Amīn Khūlī claims (*Dā'irat al-Ma'ārif al-Islāmiyya*, vol. 9, p. 412) that the confinement of Qur'anic exegesis to relating transmitted material from the Holy Prophet was due to the relative simplicity with which Muslims perceived Qur'anic interpretation; until the middle of the second/ eighth century Muslims perceived interpretation simply as understanding what the words of the Qur'an meant.

As the trend to record hadiths in writing began, those concerning Qur'anic interpretation were assigned to a separate section. Previously they had been transmitted only orally. This period witnessed a slackening in the writing of original works of Qur'anic exegesis (Dhahabī, vol. 1, pp. 145-46). In this light, the period, beginning at the end of the second/eighth century, may be described as the transformation of the oral tradition of interpretation into written literature (Ma'rifat, vol. 2, p. 14). In time, however, Qur'anic exegesis was gradually distinguished from hadith. And so the science of Qur'anic exegesis was born. Nevertheless, Qur'anic exegeses were still composed largely of hadiths and as such constituted transmitted interpretation. But this changed with Ṭabarī's Qur'anic exegesis, *Jāmi' al-Bayān 'an Ta'wīl Āyī al-Qur'an*, which proved to be a major turning point.

The critical step in the development of Qur'anic exegesis occurred in the fourth/tenth century when discussion of extrapolation started to make headway in this discipline. The systematic composition of syntax, morphology, and lexicon, the translation of philosophical works into Arabic during the 'Abbāsid caliphal dynasty the emergence of jurisprudential and theological differences, and finally the worsening of zealous sectarianism—all these helped in some way in the development of the science of Qur'anic exegesis. From this time on, Qur'anic exegeses were written in distinctive styles that set them apart. They were written from a wide range of perspectives: literary, jurisprudential, philosophical, theological, mystical, and scientific. And this trend continued into the fourteenth/twentieth. Some Qur'anic exegets strove to combine a number of these perspectives and some insisted on retaining the method of transmitted interpretation (Dhahabī, vol. 1, pp. 150-52; Ma'rifat, vol. 2, pp. 14-17). Modernity has also had its effects on the science, stimulating new methods and approaches (see below).

Qur'anic exegesis in its traditional and prevalent form considers the Qur'anic verses according to their order in the Scripture. In addition, a contemporary tendency that has gained currency, especially in Iran, is to study the meaning of the Qur'an in a thematic fashion; this style is referred to as *thematic exegesis*. This method seeks to study a particular topic in the Qur'an that is relevant to some contemporary question. For this, the exeget collects all the pertinent verses and studies them together, taking into account the commentaries and studies of earlier exegeses, and in this way hopes to obtain a Qur'anic perspective on the topic in question and its various aspects. This method is considered the most effective approach to Qur'anic exegesis in the present age (Ṣaghīr, pp. 149, 151).

Some scholars, however, have cast doubt on the innovativeness of this approach. But these scholars, it should be noted, understand thematic exegesis in a broader sense that includes any investigation of a particular Qur'anic subject or even the Qur'anic interpertation by cross-referencing its verses (Dhahabī, vol. 1, p. 153; Ma'rifat, vol. 2, p. 17; Ayāzī, p. 145; for a critique of this view, see Jalīlī, pp. 88-93).

The most significant thematic exegeses are Ja'far Subḥānī's *Mafāhīm al-Qur'an* (translated into Persian under the title *Manshūr-i Jāvīd-i Qur'an*), Jawādī Āmulī's *Tafsīr-i Mawḍū'ī*, and Makārim Shīrāzī et. al.'s *Payām-i Qur'an*. These are multivolume thematic exegeses. There are also a number of one-volume thematic exegeses examining the Qur'anic perspective on such subjects as the human being, the female, the individual and society; these appear in Persian as well as in Arabic (for further details on thematic exegeses and their methodology, see Muslim, pp. 15-17, 21- 33; Ayāzī, pp. 145-151; Jalīlī, pp. 99-163).

2. QUR'ANIC EXEGESES BY THE PROPHET

Muḥammad 'Alī Mahdavīrād

Historians consider the formative period of Islam—more accurately, the lifetime of the Prophet—as the beginning of the practice of Qur'anic exegesis. There are numerous verses in the Qur'an that define the Prophet's role as going beyond the mere conveyance of Revelation to include its interpretation, exposition, and teaching (16:44, 64, 2:151, 3:164, 62:2). The Prophet was thus the first to interpret the Qur'an. However, there is disagreement among Qur'anic exegets on determining the precise role of the Prophet in this capacity. Some have understood his function to consist of merely interpreting unclear (*mujmal*) and equivocal (*mutashābih*) verses (Fakhr Rāzī, vol. 20 p. 38; Ālūsī, vol. 14, p. 150. Others, e.g. 'Allāma Ṭabāṭabā'ī (1971-74, vol. 12, p. 261)—the contemporary Shī'a Qur'anic exeget—dismiss this view, citing 16:44.

Historical evidence seems to be in favor of the latter position. For although the Qur'an was revealed in eloquent Arabic (Ibn

Khaldūn, vol. 1, Introduction, p. 553), the Holy Prophet's (SAW) contemporaries, especially the Companions, varied radically in their grasp of Arabic literature; so much so that some were completely incapable of comprehending even its words. This was further complicated by the Qur'an's distinctive diction and method of expression. Even Arabs who could understand the literal meaning of the verses of the Qur'an were uncertain about their referents as intended by God. It was for this reason that the Prophet's Companions felt compelled to inquire the meaning of such terms as pilgrimage to Mecca (*ḥajj*), ritual prayer (*ṣalāh*), and alms tax (*zakāh*; Ibn Sa'd, vol. 2 p. 181; Ibn Ḥanbal, vol. 3, p. 318; Bukhārī Ju'fī, vol. 1, p. 155; Ṭabarī, vol. 1, p. 28; Ḥākim Nayshābūrī, vol. 2, p. 476; Quṭrubī, vol. 1, p. 39).

There is also difference of opinion among Qur'anic exegets as to what extent the Prophet interpreted the Qur'an. Ibn Taymiyya (p. 9), for instance, is convinced that the Holy Prophet provided interpretation for the entire Qur'an. To substantiate this, he cites 16:44, as well as the effort the Companions put into understanding the significance of Qur'anic verses, which would have been impossible if the meaning of the verses were unclear or incomprehensible. But other scholars, adducing a number of hadiths (Ṭabarī, vol. 1, p. 29; Quṭrubī, vol. 1, p. 31), believe that the Prophet interpreted only a small number of verses (Suyūṭī, vol. 4, pp. 196-97). Ṭabāṭabā'ī (1350 AHS/1972, p. 54) sides with the latter view, estimating the number of Prophetic hadiths interpreting Qur'anic verses to be less than two hundred and fifty. This, it seems, is not an accurate portrayal of the number of hadiths from the Prophet as an examination of the corpus of hadith would clarify. Although the number of interpretive Prophetic hadiths is restricted, the ones that help in understanding Qur'anic verses or in some way shed light on their meaning are in Abundance. This is especially the case if we take into account hadiths from the Prophet transmitted by the Prophet's Household. It needs to be pointed out that the hadiths narrated from the Prophet here are in the broad sense equivalent to the Prophetic tradition, encompassing his words, actions, and acknowledgement (*taqrīr*). As such, Qur'anic interpretation offered by the Prophet may be divided into a number of categories, as explained below:

1. Elucidating vague (*mujmal*) verses. Many injunctions set forth in the Qur'an are vague; God entrusted to the Prophet the duty to elaborate on such verses. Examples of such cases abound in various chapters of Islamic law (for Muslim jurists' explanations on such Qur'anic terms as ritual prayer (*ṣalāh*), pilgrimage to Mecca (*ḥajj*), alms tax (*zakāh*), and trade (*bay'*), see Shahīd Thānī, vol. 1, pp. 136-138, 355-356, vol. 2, pp. 6-7, 119-120, vol. 3, pp. 144-145; Muḥammad Sa'īd Manṣūr, p. 365).

2. Restricting the general (*'āmm*) verses. Prophetic Traditions confine many of the general injunctions decreed in the verses of the Qur'an. Muslims jurists in numerous cases cite hadiths from the Prophet to limit the scope of a general injunction in the Qur'an (Ibn 'Arabī, vol. 1, p. 184; Fāḍil Miqdād, vol. 2, p. 341; Shahīd Thānī, vol. 9, p. 214).

3. Delimiting the absolute (*muṭlaq*) verses. There are many verses in the Qur'an prescribing absolute decrees (e.g., 4:93, 6:82, 5:38) that prophetic Tradition delimits (Ṭabarī, vol. 7, p. 168; 'Ayyāshī, vol. 1, p. 267; Ṭūsī, vol. 3, p. 295; Quṭrubī, vol. 7, p. 3; Ṭabāṭabā'ī, 1971-74, vol. 5, p. 329).

4. Defining canonic terms. The Qur'an was revealed in Arabic to the Arabs. There were words, however, to which the Qur'an gave new meanings. These terms had to be defined by the Prophet. In addition to the aforementioned hadiths concerning such terms as ritual prayer (*ṣalāh*), pilgrimage to Mecca (*ḥajj*), and alms tax (*zakāh*), there are other transmitted and historical material recorded in the Shī'a and Sunnī corpora treating of canonic terms and phrases, such as observers of fast (*al-sā'iḥūn*, Qur'an 9:112; Ḥakim Nayshābūrī, vol. 2, p. 335; Suyūṭī, vol. 3, p. 281; Ḥuwayzī, vol. 2, p. 271) and the phrase: those who can afford the expenses (*man istaṭā'a ilayhi sabīlan*, 3:97; Ṭabarī, vol. 4, pp. 11-12; Suyūṭī, vol. 2, p. 56; Ḥuwayzī, vol. 1, p. 372).

5. Expanding on Qur'anic injunctions. Occasionally the Qur'an mentions a certain injunction in general without providing specifics. In such cases, it was upon the Prophet to elucidate on the details (Shahīd Thānī, vol. 14, pp. 362-63).

6. Distinguishing the abrogating and the abrogated verses. It is a point of debate whether any of the Qur'anic verses have been abrogated. Those, however, who argue for the presence of abrogated verses in the Qur'an consider them to be very few (Khu'ī, p. 277; Ma'rifat, vol. 2, p. 277). Acknowledgment of the accuracy of this view would entail that the Prophetic hadith may merely distinguish the abrogating verses from the abrogated ones. It is, for example, contended that verse 2:240 was abrogated by verses 2:234 and 4:12 (Suyūṭī, vol. 1, p. 573; Ḥurr 'Āmilī, vol. 22, pp. 235-239; Ḥuwayzī, vol. 1, p. 240) or that verses 4:15-16 were abrogated by verse 24:2 ('Ayyāshī, vol. 1, pp. 227-28; Ṭabarsī, vol. 3, p. 34; Ḥuwayzī, vol. 1, p. 456).

3. QUR'ANIC EXEGESES BY THE PROPHET'S HOUSEHOLD

Muḥsin Qāsimpūr

Shī'a Imams have articulated expositions in the way of Qur'anic interpretation which have been independently or dependently recorded in the works of their disciples. The Holy Qur'an (16:44) asserts that clarifying the meaning of Qur'anic verses is a duty of the Holy Prophet and after his death, according to the hadith of the two weighty things (*Thiqalayn*)—a consecutive (*mutawātir*) hadith, this duty was entrusted to his Household. Shī'as believe that the Holy Prophet unambiguously announced his Household's authority in religion and knowledge, obliging Muslims to follow them (Khu'ī, pp. 397-98). It would be an illustration of subjective interpretation (*tafsīr bi-'l-ra'y*) should an attempt be made to understand the Qur'an without recourse to the hadiths from the Prophet's Household that constitutes a comprehensive exposition of the general points of the verses of the Qur'an (ibid., p. 397).

From the Shī'a perspective, the words of the Imams carry

the same authority as those of the Holy Prophet. Provided that they be authenticated by applying the assessment principles and criteria of content and chain of transmission, the hadiths from the Prophet's Household are on a par with those from the Holy Prophet (Ṭūsī, 1376 AHS/1996, vol. 1, pp. 86-87). As indicated by the hadith narrated by Shaykh Mufīd from Imam Bāqir (p. 42), the hadiths narrated from the Prophet's Household derive, first, from the Holy Prophet and, ultimately, from God. In another hadith, Imam Sādiq describes the knowledge of the Imams as a property of the Holy Prophet inherited by them (Kulaynī, vol. 1, pp. 292-293).

To cite another hadith from Imam Bāqir, the Imams are the inheritors of the knowledge of all the prophets (Kulaynī, vol. 1, p. 231). Therefore, humanking must resort to those who possess the firm words of guidance (Kūfī, pp. 257-258). Imam 'Alī and by extension all the Imams, as explained in a hadith from Imam Sādiq ('Ayyāshī, vol. 1, p. 93), have a thorough comprehension of the meaning of the Qur'an. The solid connection between the hadiths narrated from the Prophet's Household and those from the Holy Prophet is made all the more clear by considering the hadith from Imam 'Alī regarding the point in question ('Ayyāshī, vol. 1, pp. 91-92 and Ibn Bābiwayh (1363 AHS/1985), vol. 1, pp. 284-285). According to this hadith, Imam 'Alī was personally tutored by the Holy Prophet in the knowledge of the Qur'an—its *tafsīr* and *ta'wīl*, its general (*'āmm*) and particular (*khāṣṣ*), its univocal (*muḥkam*) and equivocal (*mutashābih*), its abrogating (*nāsikh*) and abrogated (*mansūkh*).

Likewise, the authority of the hadiths narrated from the Prophet's Household is substantiated by the verses of the Qur'an as well as by hadiths. Based on the Verse of Purity (33:33), the Prophet's Household are secured against all impurities of speech and conduct, and the logical conclusion of this is the flawlessness of their discourse (Kulaynī, vol. 1, pp. 260-261). In addition, there are a number of hadiths proclaiming that the Prophet's Household are indisputably included among the People of Remembrance (*ahl al-dhikr*, Ḥaskānī, vol. 1, pp. 432-437). Likewise, 16:43 expresses the necessity of seeking the knowledge of the People of Remembrance and logically suggests the authority of the hadiths from the Prophet's Household (Ṭabāṭabā'ī's discussion on the verse in question).

The exegetic hadiths from the Prophet's Household concern mainly the content and meaning of the verses of the Qur'an. This, however, should not be construed to suggest that they neglect the literal aspect of the verses of the Qur'an ('Ayyāshī, vol. 1, p. 306; Ibn Bābiwayh, 1361 AHS/1982, p. 139). The Prophet's Household were concerned primarily with content and meaning like Qur'anic verses allowed of various interpretations. So in order to preclude misinterpretations of the Qur'an, they direct their focus toward this aspect, shedding light on how people could benefit from the meaning of the Qur'an (Ibn Bābiwayh, 1361 AHS/1982, pp. 133-134; Ma'rifat, 1418-1419/1997-1998, vol. 1, p. 469).

Imam 'Alī is enumerated among the greatest of Qur'anic exegets and considered the most knowledgeable of the Prophet's Companions on the Revelation (*tanzīl*) and interpretation (*ta'wīl*) of the Qur'an (Ḥaskānī, vol. 1, pp. 39, 47-50). Some reports related to the history of Qur'anic exegesis and interpretation point to a "Scripture of 'Alī." In this Scripture, he purportedly arranged the verses of the Qur'an in their chronological order of revelation, complementing with their *ta'wīl* and *tafsīr* and indicating the abrogating the abrogated verses (Ḥaskānī, vol. 1, pp. 36-38; Majlisī, vol. 89, p. 40). Moreover, there are passages in *Nahj al-Balāgha* that either directly or indirectly treat of the meaning of the verses of the Qur'an (for further details on such passages, see Muṣṭafawī, pp. 39-150).

The Imams succeeding Imam 'Alī took up the intra-textual method of interpretation (*tafsīr al-Qur'an bi-'l-Qur'an*) while shedding light on the deeper, esoteric meaning of the words of the Qur'an (Ṣaffār Qummī, p. 196). Imams Ḥasan and Ḥusayn did not found a new hermeneutical school, though there are occasional reports of their interpreting the Qur'an (Ibn

Bābiwayh, 1410/1989, p. 131; 'Imād al-Dīn Ṭabarī, pp. 240-241).

There are a number of historical texts indicating Imam Sajjād's practice of exegesis in the hermeneutical school of Medina. Furthermore, his *al-Ṣaḥīfa al-Sajjādiyya*, along with his other supplications, in essence amounts to an exegesis and exposition of certain passages of the Qur'an. In this book, Imam Sajjād employs verses of the Qur'an, alludes to and cites them, while borrowing from the Qur'an in other ways as well (*al-Ṣaḥīfa al-Sajjādiyya*, Pers. tr., pp. 141, 147, 271, 283, 285). The exposition of the "righteous servants [of God]" in the forty fourth supplication, on the occasion of the commencement of the holy month of Ramaḍān, is one such instance (pp. 282-293). A number of hadiths are related from him concerning the greatness of the Qur'an (Kulaynī, vol. 2, pp. 605, 609, 612) and the occasions of revelation of certain verses (Kūfī, pp. 125, 153-154, 159-160, 366). In expounding on some verses of the Qur'an, Imam Sajjād indicates that the Imams are the interpretation and the transcendent reality of these verses (Kūfī, p. 314; Ibn Bābiwayh, 1361 AHS/1982, p. 298; Ḥaskānī, vol. 1, p. 130).

Imam Bāqir's exegetic hadiths were compiled by one of his disciples, Abū al-Jārūd Ziyād ibn Mundhir (Ibn Nadīm, Pers. tr., p. 59; also see al-Bāqir, Imam Muḥammad ibn Alī). Imam Bāqir's hadiths provide explanations for the difficult phrases and clauses of some Qur'anic verses as well as for certain terms by citing other verses of the Qur'an, which is in essence the intra-textual method of exegesis (e.g. 'Ayyāshī, vol. 1, p. 150 ff). In addition, these hadiths also interpret certain verses as signifying events that would befall the Imams in the future ('Ayyāshī, vol. 3, p. 37; Kulaynī, vol. 1, pp. 251-252). There are also other instances where Imam Bāqir expounds on the abrogating and abrogated verses and on the jurisprudential aspect of God's words ('Ayyāshī, vol. 1, p. 377; Kulaynī, vol. 5, p. 360; Ibn Bābiwayh 1401/1980, vol. 1, pp. 278-279).

Numerous hadiths from Imam Sādiq concerning a wide range of Qur'anic topics are dispersed throughout a number of books ('Ayyāshī, vol. 1, pp. 108, 113, 176; Ibn Bābiwayh, 1357 AHS/1978, pp. 92-93, 149, 154-155, 157-158; for the work of Qur'anic exposition attributed to him, see Imam Ja'far Sādiq's Exegesis of the Qur'an).

Among topics treated in the exegetic hadiths from the Prophet's Household, one may point to expositions of verses of the revealed prescripts (*āyāt al-aḥkām*) and the replies to questions on religious practice. In addition to the intra-textual practice of exegesis, the Imams on certain occasions ascribed their exegesis to the Prophet or other Imams ('Ayyāshī, vol. 1, pp. 312, 358). Other Imams, i.e. Imam Kāẓim, Imam Riḍā, and Imam Hādī, took up the interpretative method of their predecessors; i.e., exegesis by way of intra-textual understanding ('Ayyāshī, vol. 1, pp. 121, 133, 202, 386). But they also occasionally ascribed an exegesis to the Prophet or the preceding Infallibles ('Ayyāshī, vol. 1, pp. 199, 135) - an interpretative method that may be designated as transmitted hermeneutics. Moreover, there are other occasions where the Imams offer objective instances for certain verses ('Ayyāshī, vol. 1, pp. 281, 392) or expositions for difficult phrases ('Ayyāshī, vol. 1, p. 232).

Based on some historical accounts, a number of disciples of the Imams—some of whom lived long enough to be acquainted with more than one Imam—authored works of Qur'anic exegesis. However, of the many such exegeses, all are lost and only fragmentary quotations remain in the Shī'a sources. Najāshī and Shaykh Ṭūsī enumerate a number of these works (Najāshī, pp. 11, 15-16, 78, 89, 128, 145, 217, 240, 252, 260; Shaykh Ṭūsī, 1420/2000, pp. 14, 83, 116, 122) on the discussions pertaining to the studies of Shī'a authorities of transmission (*rijāl*). The most prominent of these lost works are the exegeses by Abān ibn Taghlib (d. 141/758-759), a disciple of the Imams Sajjād, Bāqir, and Sādiq (Najāshī, p. 10), and Abū Ḥamza Thābit ibn Dīnār Thumālī (d. 150/767-768), also an intimate companion of the same three Imams (Najāshī, pp. 115, 116). Aḥmad ibn Muḥammad Tha'lab (d. 427/1035-1036) in his own work of Qur'anic exegesis quotes from Abū Ḥamza Thumālī's (e.g., vol. 1, p. 82, vol. 8, p. 117, vol. 9, p. 135).

The names of some early works of Shī'a exegesis on the Qur'an, in which the exegetic hadiths from the Imam are recorded, include: the exegesis attributed to Imam Ḥasan al-'Askarī, the exegesis by 'Alī ibn Ibrāhīm al-Qummī (fl. c. 307/919-920), the exegesis by Furāt Kūfī, and that by 'Ayyāshī. As Ṭabarsī explains (vol. 1, p. 75), Shī'a exegeses prior to Shaykh Ṭūsī are all in the genre of transmitted exegesis, confined to the compilation of hadiths from the Prophet's Household.

It seems as though one of the favourite areas which the disciples of the Imams engaged in was recording hadiths that determined the occasion of revelation of verses as relating to the Prophet's Household. Muḥammad Riḍā Ḥusaynī in his foreword to al-Ḥibarī's exegesis (pp. 146-152) provides a list of the works thus inclined. The earliest work of this type is *Kitāb Mā Nuzzila min al-Qur'an fī 'Alī 'alayhi al-Salām* by Ḥusayn ibn Ḥakam Ḥibarī (d. 286/899). This work was published by Sayyid Aḥmad Ishkiwarī with this title in Baghdad (1398/1977-1978); Muḥammad Riḍā Ḥusaynī, however, has published it under the title *Tafsīr al-Ḥibarī* in Beirut (1408/1987-1988). Another such work is *Ta'wīl Mā Nuzzila min al-Qur'an al-Karīm fī al-Nabī wa Ālih Ṣalla Allāh 'alayhim* by Muḥammad ibn 'Abbās ibn Māhyār, known as Ibn Juḥām (fl. c. 328/939-940), which Fāris Tabrīzīyān Ḥassūn reconstructed based on reports and quotations attested in later sources (Qum 1420/1999-2000). Muḥammad ibn 'Abd al-Karīm Shahristānī (d. 548/1153-1154), influenced by his teacher Abū al-Qāsim Sulaymān ibn Nāṣir Anṣārī (d. 512/1118-1119), drew on the interpretations by the Prophet's Household in his exegesis *Mafātīḥ al-Asrār wa Maṣābīḥ al-Abrār* (vol. 1, pp. 105-106).

4. EXEGESES BY THE COMPANIONS

'Alīriḍā Bahārdūst

Of the Prophet's Companions, ten are recognised as Qur'anic exegets: the four caliphs, 'Abd Allāh ibn Mas'ūd, 'Abd Allāh ibn 'Abbās, Ubayy ibn Ka'b, Zayd ibn Thābit, Abū Mūsā Ash'arī, and 'Abd Allāh ibn Zubayr (Suyūṭī 1363 AHS/1383, vol. 4, p. 233). Suyūṭī (ibid.) considers 'Alī ibn Abī Ṭālib as surpassing the other caliphs, who died far earlier, in the quantity of interpretative explanations he produced. Muḥammad Ḥusayn Dhahabī (vol. 1, pp. 64-65) offers a further reason, namely, that the first three caliphs were preoccupied with the crucial affairs of the state and engrossed by Muslims' conquests, whereas during this period, 'Alī was relatively free. Dhahabī (vol. 1 p.65) goes further to expound on Suyūṭī's reasoning by saying that 'Alī lived long enough to satisfy the dire need of the Muslims for Qur'anic interpretation. Furthermore, he states that only four of the ten Companions mentioned above —'Alī ibn Abī Ṭālib, 'Abd Allāh ibn 'Abbās, 'Abd Allāh ibn Mas'ūd, and

Ubayy ibn Ka'b—produced a significant amount of Qur'anic exegesis; from the other six, only a few exegetic hadiths have been preserved.

Zarkashī (vol. 2, p. 293) considers 'Alī as the most outstanding Qur'anic exeget among the Companions. He assigns second place to Ibn 'Abbās. According to Zarkashī, although Ibn 'Abbās derived his knowledge of Qur'anic exegesis from 'Alī, the quantity recorded from him is greater even than that from 'Alī.

Imam 'Alī is distinguished by the honorary title of the most distinguished of the exegets (*ṣadr al-mufassirīn*). His Qur'anic exegesis was generally accepted by the other Companions (*Muqaddimatān*, "Muqaddima Ibn 'Aṭiyya," p. 262; Quṭrubī, vol. 1, p. 35; Tha'ālibī, vol. 1, p. 141). That Imam 'Alī was the most knowledgeable Companion concerning the meaning of the Qur'an, the occasions of revelation of its verses, and the science of *tafsīr* and *ta'wīl* is universally accepted by all Muslims (Muḥammad Ḥusayn Dhahabī, vol. 1, pp. 89-90). In Shī'a hadiths, Imam 'Alī is referred to as the speaking Word of God (*kalām Allāh al-nāṭiq*; Ibn Bābiwayh, vol. 2, p. 49; Majlisī, vol. 30, p. 546, vol. 79, p. 199). Imam 'Alī was raised and nurtured in the Prophet's house, thus receiving the knowledge of the Prophet directly from himself (Muḥammad Ḥusayn Dhahabī, vol. 1, pp. 89; *Nahj al-Balāgha*, Sermon 192). Ibn 'Abbās—who was undoubtedly an associate and disciple of 'Alī (Ibn Abī al-Ḥadīd, vol. 1, p. 19) and who derived the greater part of his knowledge of Qur'anic exegesis from him (*Muqaddimatān*, "Muqaddima Ibn 'Aṭiyya," p. 263)—compares his knowledge to 'Alī's as a drop of rain in a boundless ocean (Ibn Abī al-Ḥadīd, vol. 1, p. 19).

The Prophet of God on many occasions affirmed the concurrence of the Qur'an and 'Alī and their inseparability (Ḥākim Nayshābūrī, 1406/1985, vol. 3, pp. 124-127). It is reported that Imam 'Alī would often urge Muslims to ask him about the Qur'an: Ask me concerning God's book (*salūnī 'an kitāb Allāh*; Ibn Sa'd, vol. 2, p. 338; Balādhurī, p. 99; Ibn 'Asākir, vol. 27, p. 100, vol. 42, p. 398; Ibn Ḥajar 'Asqalānī, *Fatḥ al-Bārī*, vol.

11, p. 249). Furthermore, he would say that there is no verse in the Qur'an which he had not memorised and learned its interpretation from the Holy Prophet (Iskāfī, pp. 300-3001); he swore that he knew the persons about whom the verses were revealed and the locations where they were revealed (Akhṭab Khwārazm, p. 90; Muttaqī, vol. 13, p. 128).

Ibn Mas'ūd describes 'Alī as the most knowledgeable person after the Prophet (Ibn Ṭāwūs, p. 558; Majlisī, vol. 89, p. 105) with knowledge of the esoteric and the exoteric aspects of the Qur'an (Ibn 'Asākir, vol. 42, p.400; Tha'ālibī, vol. 1, p. 53; for further details onthe status and importance of 'Alī regarding Qur'anic exegesis, see Interpretation by the Prophet's Household).

The most prominent Companion in the discipline of Qur'anic exegesis following 'Alī ibn Abī Ṭālib is 'Abd Allāh ibn 'Abbās. He was praised by the Companions and later Muslims as the interpretation of the Qur'an (*tarjumān al-Qur'an*; Ibn Ḥajar 'Asqalānī, *Fatḥ al-Bārī*, vol. 7, p. 171, vol. 8, p. 157; Ibn Ḥajar 'Asqalānī, *al-Iṣāba*, vol. 2, p. 332), clearly demonstrating his prominence in Qur'anic *tafsīr* and *ta'wīl*. He was raised largely by the Holy Prophet and was persistently in the Holy Prophet's company when he was no more than in his adolescence, thus witnessing many of the events that occasioned the revelation of Qur'anic verses (Muhammad Ḥusayn Dhahabī, vol. 1, p. 68). Traditions narrated from companions reveal that the Holy Prophet prayed that he should grow to become learned in Islamic knowledge and *ta'wīl* of the Qur'an and seeped in wisdom (Ibn Ḥajar 'Asqalānī, *al-Iṣāba*, vol. 1, p. 89). Other companions confirm that Imam 'Alī also maintained this and acknowledged his knowledge of Qur'anic exegesis (*Muqaddimatān*, Ibn 'Aṭiyya's Introduction; Quṭrubī, vol. 1, p. 35).

Ibn 'Abbās endeavoured to make Qur'anic exegesis his main purpose following the Prophet's death. In order to compensate for what he had missed during the Holy Prophet's life due to his tender age, he resolved to seek the knowledge of Qur'anic interpretation from the eminent Companions (Muḥammad

Husayn Dhahabī, vol. 1, pp. 68-69; for the names of the Companions with whom he studied, see Quṭrubī, vol. 1, p. 26; Suyūṭī, 1404/1982, vol. 6, p. 242).

In addition to reflecting on the content of the Qur'an (Ṭabarī, vol. 24, p. 31; Suyūṭī, 1404/1982, vol. 5, p. 347), studying the exegetic hadiths narrated from the Holy Prophet, and considering the occasions of revelation (Quṭrubī, vol. 1, p. 26; Suyūṭī, 1404/1982, vol. 6, 242), Ibn 'Abbās brought also his knowledge of Arabic literature, lexicography, and eloquence of speech to weigh on his reading of the Qur'anic verses. The most celebrated example of Ibn 'Abbās' exegetic discussions consists of his answers to questions posed by Nāfi' ibn Azraq (Suyūṭī, 1363 AHS/1983, vol. 2, pp. 68-105).

One controversial question raised concerning Ibn 'Abbās' exegesis is his recourse to the People of the Book, i.e., Christians and Jews, in understanding the meaning of the Qur'an and determining its limits. Ma'rifat (vol. 1, pp. 252-267) dismisses this account citing a number of reports, and Muḥammad Husayn Dhahabī (vol. 1, p. 71) claims that such recourse was limited to only a few instances (see below).

Ibn 'Abbās defines four levels of Qur'anic understanding: 1. that which Arabs can grasp on account of their native language, 2. that which all Muslims are obliged to know, such as the verses decreeing what is permissible and what is forbidden, 3. that which is accessible only to the scholars, and 4. that which is merely confined to God, e.g. the ambiguous verses (*mutashābihāt*; Ṭabarī, vol. 1, p. 26).

Ibn 'Abbās' method of exegesis was incorporated into the exegetic school of Mecca (Muḥammad Husayn Dhahabī, vol. 1, pp. 70, 102). But his fame in Qur'anic exegesis also led to the false attribution of certain exegeses to him (Ṣāwī Juwaynī, p. 41). So much so that there is exegesis related from him concerning every verse of the Qur'an. This has caused critics to view the large volume of exegesis attributed to him with skepticism (Muḥammad Husayn Dhahabī, vol. 1, p. 77). It may be for this reason that Shāfiʿī verifies only around one hundred of the exegetic comments attributed to Ibn ʿAbbās (Suyūtī, 1363 AHS/1983, vol. 4, p. 239). To distinguish between authentic and inauthentic reports, a number of contemporary scholars have felt compelled to analyse the chains of transmission of the reports ostensibly narrated on the authority of Ibn ʿAbbās (Muḥammad Ḥusayn Dhahabī, vol. 1, pp. 77-81; Maʿrifat, vol. 1, pp. 268-295). Several books of exegesis are ascribed to Ibn ʿAbbās (Ibn Nadīm, Pers. tr., p. 36; Aqā Buzurg Tihrānī vol. 4, p. 270), the most well-known being *Tanwīr al-Miqbās min Tafsīr Ibn ʿAbbās* (to learn more about this book and its authenticity, see Muḥammad Ḥusayn Dhahabī, vol. 1, p. 82; Maʿrifat, vol. 1, p. 297; Ibn ʿAbbās's Exegesis).

ʿAbd Allāh ibn Masʿūd is also classified among the first generation Qurʾanic exegets. He was recognised as a scholar of the meaning of the Qurʾan and the occasions of revelation of its verses (Ibn Taymiyya, p. 40). He was diligent in his pursuit to understand the meaning of the verses and their practical application (ibid., p. 40-41) and in his commitment to the discipline of Qurʾanic exegesis (Abū Nuʿaym, vol. 1, pp. 124-139). He is considered the founder of Kufa's school of exegesis (Muḥammad Ḥusayn Dhahabī, vol. 1, p. 120 and Rāmyār, p. 355).

According to Ibn Kathīr (*Tafsīr al-Qurʾan al-ʿAẓīm*, vol. 1, p. 8) Sudda quotes abundantly in his exegesis from Ibn Masʿūd. His exegeses on the Qurʾan later influenced exegets from a variety of schools and denominations (e.g. Ṭūsī, vol. 1 p. 57 and Zamakhsharī, vol. 1 p. 38). Muḥammad Ḥusayn Dhahabī (vol. 1, pp. 87-88) verifies all the chains of transmission from Ibn Masʿūd excepting that which is through Abū Rawq and Ḍaḥḥāk.

Another eminent Qurʾanic exeget of this era is Ubayy ibn Kaʿb. He is enumerated among the scribes the Holy Prophet employed for writing down the Qurʾan as it was revealed (Ibn Shuʿba, p. 428; Ibn Kathīr, *al-Bidāya wa al-Nihāya*, vol. 5, p. 362; Ṭabarsī, vol. 1, Aḥmad Riḍā's introduction, p. 69). Due to his prominent status in the discipline of Qurʾanic recitation (*qirā'a*), he was given the epithet Master of Reciters (*sayyid al-qurrā'*; Ibn Kathīr, *al-Bidāya wa al-Nihāya*, vol. 3, p. 383, vol. 5, p. 362, vol. 7, p. 110; Ibn Hajar 'Asqalānī, *al-Iṣāba*, vol. 1, p. 19, vol. 2, p. 237, vol. 4, p. 470). As reported by Abū al-'Ālīya, when Abū Bakr assembled a number of the scribes of the Qur'an to standardise the text of the Qur'an, Ubayy ibn Ka'b was granted the honour of dictating it to them (Sijistānī, p. 15). And at the time of 'Uthmān, he figured largely in the project to compile Uthmān's standardised text (ibid., p. 33). He is considered by some to be the precursor in compiling works in the genre of the merits of the Qur'an (*faḍā'il al-qur'an*; Ibn Nadīm, Pers. tr., p. 39; Āqā Buzurg Ṭihrānī, vol. 16, p. 262; Ṣadr, p. 319). Suyūṭī (1363 AHS/1983, vol. 4, p. 240) reports from Ubayy ibn Ka'b about a voluminous Qur'anic exegesis transmitted on the authority of Abū Ja'far Rāzī, Rabī' ibn Anas, and Abū al-'Ālīya, that Ṭabarī and Ibn Abī Hātam in their exegeses and Hākim in *al-Mustadrak*, and Ahmad ibn Hanbal in *Musnad* all quoted from this source.

Without doubt, the Companions were serious in their effort to understand the Qur'an and to confirm their practice thereto (Ṭabarī, vol. 1, p. 27). Nevertheless, the Companions differed in their knowledge of the Qur'an, Arabic literature, intellectual capacity, and the duration of their companionship with the Prophet (Muhammad Husayn Dhahabī, vol. 1, pp. 36-38). This may be inferred from the numerous accounts where some Companions confessed their ignorance of the meaning of a Qur'anic verse. When asked of the meaning of *wa fākiha wa abbā* in 80:31, Abū Bakr could only concede ignorance (Suyūṭī, 1363 AHS/1983, vol. 2, p. 4). The Second Caliph, too, expressed doubt as to the meaning of the word *abbā* in this verse. On another occasion, the Second Caliph asked others for the meaning of *takhawwuf* in 16:47. Ibn 'Abbās once suggested that he realised the meaning of *fāṭir al-samāwāt* (35:1) only after witnessing a quarrel between two Bedouin (Muhammad Husayn Dhahabī, vol. 1, pp. 37-38). From these accounts, we may infer the status of the other Companions as well.

Following the Holy Prophet's demise, some Companions avoided engaging in Qur'anic exegesis (*Muqaddimatān, Muqaddima Kitāb al-Mabānī*, pp. 183-184). This seems to have been related to the established policy of the caliphate to forbid the publication and dissemination of Prophetic hadiths, for in that period Qur'anic exegesis consisted largely of the exegetic Prophetic hadiths. During the Holy Prophet's life, the Companions would record in their manuscripts the revealed verses along with the Prophet's exposition ('Askarī, vol. 2, p. 414). But due to the policy dictated during the standardisation of the Qur'anic scripture to divest all initial manuscripts of their exegetic and extra-Qur'anic material and due to the harsh reaction that asking questions regarding the Qur'an would elicit (Suyūṭī, 1363 AHS/1983, vol. 3, pp. 8-9), Muslims tended to content themselves with the perfunctory reading of the Qur'an (Muḥammad ibn Aḥmad Dhahabī, vol. 1, p. 7).

During the period of the Companions, Qur'anic exegesis was no more than a branch of the discipline of hadith, as it consisted in narrating exegetic hadiths. (They did, of course, consider philology to weigh on understanding the individual words of the Qur'an.) It may be for this reason that Ibn Taymiyya (p. 10) claims that the Companions rarely disagreed on Qur'anic exegesis. This period of Qur'anic exegesis may be characterised by its simplicity and lack of complexity, the complacence not to go beyond the literal meaning of the verses, the inclination to avoid thorough examination of the Qur'anic phrases, and the confinement of the practice of exegesis to the ambiguous verses as opposed to studying all the verses. Noteworthy to say that in the period of the Companions, Qur'anic exegesis was not committed to writing, although a number of Companions had included some of the Holy Prophet's expositions in their manuscripts (*Muqaddimatān*, Muqaddima Kitāb al-Mabānī, p. 193; for further details on this period of Qur'anic exegesis, see Muḥammad Ḥusayn Dhahabī, vol. 1, pp. 97-98; Shahḥāta, pp. 93-94; Ma'rifat, vol. 1, pp. 307-309; Abū Ṭabara, pp. 44-45).

The main sources from which the Companions derived exegetic insight were (1) the Qur'an itself (Ṭabarī, vol. 9, pp. 28-29, vol. 24 p.31; Ṭūsī, vol. 5, p. 121; Suyūṭī, 1404/1982, vol. 5, p. 347, (2) expositions from the Holy Prophet, which they may have heard directly from the Holy Prophet or through other Companions, and (3) their personal inference. In interpreting the Qur'an, they relied on their personal understanding and took into consideration the context provided by pre-Islamic Arab culture and other existing cultures (Muḥammad Ḥusayn Dhahabī, vol. 1, pp. 59-61). In defining the meaning of a particular word, some Companions would cite pre-Islamic poetry (e.g. Suyūṭī, 1363 AHS/1983, vol. 2, pp. 67-105), though there have been disagreements among scholars as to whether such citation is credible (Suyūṭī, 1363 AHS/1983, vol. 2, p. 67; Niẓām al-A'raj, vol. 1, p. 16). Ibn 'Abbās and the Second Caliph would refer to pre-Islamic poetry as the Arabs' collection of poetry (*dīwān*; Suyūṭī, 1363 AHS/1983, vol. 2, p. 67; Shātibī, vol. 2, p. 88). Another piece of evidence that the Companions arrived at their exegeses, at least in part, based on their personal inference is their disagreements, some of which have been recorded (Kulaynī, vol. 1, pp. 62-64). Ibn Taymiyya (p. 37), however, asserts that their disagreements were limited.

Generally speaking, the exegeses generated by the Companions may be classified into two categories: continuous (*marfū'*) and discontinuous (*mawqūf*). continuous, in the science of hadithology, denotes a hadith that is ultimately traced back to the Prophet (Ibn Ṣalāḥ, p. 122) and can be accepted as a Prophetic hadith. Suyūṭī (1363 AHS/1983, vol. 4, p. 208) deems the verifiable continuous hadiths as limited in number; he enumerates two hundred and fifty such hadiths in his *al-Itqān* (vol. 4, pp. 244-298). But as regards the credibility of discontinuous hadiths—those that express the Companions' personal opinions rather than those of the Holy Prophet (Ibn Ṣalāḥ, p. 123)—there is disagreement between Sunnī and Shī'a scholars. Shī'a exegets, though occasionally citing the views of the Companions, do not consider them self-sufficient proof (Ṭabāṭabā'ī, vol. 3, p. 84). Among the Sunnīs, Ḥākim Nayshābūrī's dictum in *al-Mustadrak* (vol. 2, p. 258, 263) constituted the basis on which Sunnīs espoused an absolute approval of the views of the Companions. Elsewhere, however, Ḥākim Nayshabūrī (1397/1977, pp. 19-20) states that discontinuous hadiths from the Companions are credible only when they are concerned with occasions of revelation. Ibn Ṣalāḥ (p. 128) and Nawawī (p. 34) approve the latter view, for in such cases, they are not drawing personal inferences, but are rather reporting an event they witnessed (Muḥammad Ḥusayn Dhahabī, vol. 1, pp. 94-96).

Another exegetic source, considered merely second to others, is the wisdom of the People of the Book, i.e., Jews and Christians. Some Companions understood the Qur'anic verse "ask the people of the reminder (*dhikr*)" (21:7) as indicating the believers of previous religions and denominations or those informed of their ways (e.g. Zamakhsharī and Ṭabarsī). Based on this assumption, they believed that the interpretations furnished by the People of the Book might be relied upon, though only in limited instances and on the condition that they did not conflict with the Islamic doctrine. Thus, concerning the stories of previous prophets, which get only a brief treatment in the Qur'an, they would refer to the Old and New Testaments, wherein these stories are covered at length (Muḥammad Ḥusayn Dhahabī, vol. 1, pp. 62-63). Ma'rifat (vol. 1, pp. 252-253) is of the opinion that the hadith "you may speak of the Children of Israel without incurring guilt," assuming, of course, that it is an authentic Prophetic hadith, pertains to such stories. Muḥammad Ḥusayn Dhahabī (vol. 1, pp. 73-74), in concurrence with Ibn Ḥajar 'Asqalānī (*Fatḥ al-Bārī*, vol. 13, p. 282), furnishes arguments reconciling the above-quoted hadith with another Prophetic hadith saying, "Approve not of the People of the Book nor refute them."

5. THE QUR'ANIC EXEGESIS OF THE SUCCESSORS

Muḥammad Kāẓim Raḥmatī

The origin and development of Qur'anic exegesis coincided with the formation and development of the sciences of rhetoric and theology. When compared with the time of the Companions, no particular changes in the field of Qur'anic exegesis and its conservation can be seen during the time of the Successors, primarily due to the fact that these disciplines were still in their early stages (Rūmī, p. 30); the only exception being the traces of theological discussions observed in the works of the Successors. Khuḍayrī (vol. 2, pp. 785-844) compiled some of the opinions of the Successors regarding hermeneutical interpretations of the ambiguous verses as well as theological issues. Naturally, the sources mention the schools of exegesis in Iraq, Medina, and Mecca, depending upon the place or residence of the Successors (Ḥasan Baṣrī, epilogue of Muḥammad ʿAbd al-Raḥīm, vol. 2, p. 451; Jūda Muḥammad Mahdī, pp. 108-114; Abū Ḥujr, pp. 40-43). Mujāhid ibn Jabr Makkī (d. 104/722), ʿAṭāʾ ibn Abī Rabāḥ

(d. 114/732), Sa'īd ibn Jubayr (d. 95/713), and 'Ikrima Mawlā ibn 'Abbās (d. 105/723) have been identified as the forerunners of Qur'anic exegesis in Mecca (Dhahabī, vol. 1, pp. 107-118; Jūda Muḥammad Mahdī, pp. 108-111; Abū Ḥujr, pp. 41-42). Among the books of hadiths, the most important work containing the hermeneutic opinions of the Successors is al-*Jāmi' al-Saḥīḥ* by Muḥammad ibn Ismā'īl Bukhārī. For the most part, he brought in hermeneutic sayings from the Successors as narrated on the authority of Ibn 'Abbās' students (Abū Ḥujr, p. 42). These students closely followed the same manner of Qur'anic exegesis as that of Ibn 'Abbās himself (Ibid, pp. 41-42; Ṣāwī Juwaynī, pp. 25-36; also see the Ibn 'Abbās' Exegesis).

The leading figures of Qur'anic exegesis in Medina include Abū al-'Ālīya Rufay' ibn Mihrān Rīyāḥī (d. 93/711) and Muḥammad ibn Ka'b Quraẓī (d. 108/726). As for the forerunners of Qur'anic exegesis in Iraq, mention may be made of Ḥasan Baṣrī (d. 110/728), Qatāda ibn Di'āma Sadawsī (d. 118/736), Masrūq ibn Ajda' ibn Mālik Hamdānī (d. 63/682) and 'Āmir ibn Sharāḥīl Sha'bī (Dhahabī, vol. 1, pp. 118-130; Jūda Muḥammad Mahdī, pp. 111-114). The Successors of Medina had received Qur'anic exegesis either directly or indirectly from Ubayy ibn Ka'b (Abū Ḥujr, p. 42), whereas the Tābi'īn of Iraq were influenced by 'Abd Allāh ibn Mas'ūd. Of their qualities was their overwhelming reliance on opinions (*ra'ī*) and independent reasoning (*ijtihād*) in their exegeses (Ibid., p. 43). They also seemed to pay less attention to the transmitted stories of the People of the Book (*ahl al-kitāb*; ibid.).

One of the other religious centres during the period of the Successors was Khurasan, and its most prominent Successors exeget was a man by the name of Ḍaḥḥāk ibn Muzāḥim Hilālī (d. 105/723; 'Uṭwān, p. 56). Ḍaḥḥāk's method of Qur'anic exegesis was narrational (*riwā'ī*) and was based on the Prophetic narrations as well as the sayings of the Companions; moreover, due to his expertise in philology and grammar, he developed a particularised form of Qur'anic exegesis (ibid., p.60).

The sources of Qur'anic exegesis during the time of the Successors included: traditions of biblical origin (*Isrā'īliyāt*), Prophetic traditions, and the views of the Companions; occasionally it also included independent reasonings based on individual opinion (*ra'y*) and the exegesis of the Qur'an through the Qur'an (Rūmī, pp. 31-32). The exegesis of the Successors is in essence, narrational, while having sectarian and opinionated tendencies (Dhahabī, vol. 1, p. 134). Referring to these instances, Khuḍayrī (vol. 2, pp. 608-743) has presented examples and evidence for each one of them, mentioning the difference of opinions amongst the Successors when following these sources. The most important of the narrators traditions of biblical origin during this time were 'Abd Allāh ibn Salām, Ka'b al-Aḥbār, Wahb ibn Munabbih, and 'Abd al-Malik ibn Jurayj (Rūmī, p. 32; Khuḍayrī, vol. 2, p. 907). Khuḍayrī (vol. 2, pp. 884-889) also recollected various perspectives of the Successors regarding the traditions of biblical origin. In fact, one of the particularities of the Successors of Mecca was their ease in narrating from the traditions of biblical origin (Ibid., vol. 2, p. 885).

Authorities have a difference of opinion when it comes to accepting the authenticity of the Qur'anic exegeses of the Successors as well as their sayings (Ibn Qayyim Jawziyya, vol. 4, pp. 155-156; Dhahabī, vol. 1, p. 131; Abū Ḥujr, pp. 44-45; Khuḍayrī, vol. 1, pp. 49-51). Aḥmad ibn Ḥanbal and 'Abd Allāh ibn Muḥammad ibn 'Aqīl did not deem it necessary to refer to the hermeneutical opinions of the Successors (Jūda Muḥammad Mahdī, p. 115; Rūmī, p. 33). These scholars had several reasons for their position, including: 1. the fact that the Successors had not heard from the Holy Prophet directly, 2. their absence during the revelation of the Qur'anic verses, and 3. the uncertainty with regards to their impartiality (*'adāla*; Dhahabī, ibid.; Rūmī, pp. 33-34). In this respect, Abū Ḥanīfa places himself on the same level as the Successors (Dhahabī, Ibid.). At the same time, however, Aḥmad ibn Ḥanbal has been quoted permitting the use of consulting the exegesis of the Successors – the reason for this being their association and interaction with the Companions as the authorities through whom they derived hermeneutical interpretations (Ibid.; Rūmī, p. 34). This view has been accepted by most Qur'anic exegets. In fact, Ibn Taymiyya (p. 46) goes further, suggesting that if the Successors are unanimous on an issue, accepting their view becomes obligatory; but in the event that they disagree, then their view is not authoritative on any matter. Dhahabī (vol. 1, p. 132) has also preferred this opinion.

According to what Aḥmad ibn Muḥammad Tha'labī (d. 427/1035) has related, the collected sayings of the Successors such as the exegeses of 'Ikrima, Mujāhid, al-Ḥasan al-Baṣrī, Muḥammad ibn Ka'b Qurazī, and Sa'īd ibn Musayyib existed during his time, and was occasionally transmitted via more than one chain (vol. 1, pp. 76-79, 82-83). One of the narrational exegeses extensively quoting the opinions of the Successors is Ṭabarī's exegesis entitled *Jāmi' al-Bayān fī Tafsīr al-Qur'an* (Rūmī, p. 145; also see Ṭabarī's *Exegesis*). To a large extent, Khuḍayrī (vol. 1, pp. 57-82) made known the most important authorities who have narrated the sayings of the Successors.

Of the written exegeses left by the Successors, no independent text remains apart from the exegesis of Mujāhid ibn Jabr, and that too includes seemingly merely a selection of his hermeneutic views. They were chosen and compiled by Muḥammad ibn 'Abd al-Malik ibn Ḥasan, commonly known as Ibn Khayrūn (d. 539/1144; Nawfal, p. 313). Of the efforts to reconstruct the exegeses of the Successors, the reconstructed exegeses of Sa'īd ibn Jubayr and al-Ḥasan al-Baṣrī can be mentioned.

A number of Orientalists have doubted the authenticity of the Successors' Qur'anic exegeses. The most important grounds are the narrations denouncing the permissibility of Qur'anic exegesis which Ṭabarī (d. 310/922, vol. 1, pp. 29-30) has related on the authority of a number of the Successors and the Companions. At the same time, however, numerous exegetic narrations have been transmitted from these very individuals (Rippin, p. 227). Examining the sources of these narrations reveals that their narrators were primarily from Medina, and hence could only have reflected the exegetic views of some of the Companions and the Successors of Medina. A number of exegets, relying on other narrations, have commented on the permissibility and impermissibility of hermeneutical interpretation (Ṭabarī, vol. 1, pp. 30-31; *Muqaddimatān fī 'Ulūm al-Qur'an*, pp. 183-206). The most detailed and important research regarding the Qur'anic exegeses of the Successors is conducted by Muḥammad ibn 'Abd Allāh ibn 'Alī Khuḍayrī.

6. TRANSMITTED EXEGESIS

Muḥammad ʿAlī Mahdavīrād

Tafsīr ma'thūr or transmitted interpretation is a method of Qur'anic exegesis that is based on the hadiths from the Holy Prophet and, in Sunnism the elucidations reported from the Companions and, according to one view, the Successors. In Shīʿism, this method of exegesis draws on the hadiths from the Holy Prophet and the Infallibles to the exclusion of the explanations furnished by the Companions. There is a lack of agreement among scholars as to the precise definition of *tafsīr ma'thūr*. Some historians of Qur'anic exegesis (Dhahabī, 1409/1988, vol. 1, p. 154; Ṣaghīr, p. 55) include Intra-textual exegesis as well, i.e., they interpret one verse by recourse to other verses, as opposed to citing external material. But considering the literal meaning of *athar*, i.e., the root from which *ma'thūr* derives (Farāhīdī, vol. 8, p. 236 Murtaḍā Zabīdī, vol. 10, p. 13) and its technical meaning (Tahānawī, vol. 1, p. 65; Qāsimī, p. 62), it seems unlikely that intra-textual interpretation could be classified as a category of transmitted interpretation.

Qur'anic exegets unanimously believe that one of the aspects of the Holy Prophet's ministry, in addition to conveying Revelation, was to interpret and clarify the Divine Word (Interpretation by the Holy Prophet). Qur'anic exegets view 16:44, 64 as indicating this function of the Holy Prophet (Ṭūsī, vol. 6, p. 398; Fakhr Rāzī, vol. 20, p. 57; Ṭabāṭabā'ī, vol. 12, p. 284; Ibn 'Āshūr, vol. 14, p. 196). From this they draw the conclusion that the Prophetic hadiths, when proven authentic, can serve as one of the most effective means in Qur'anic exegesis (Ibn 'Āshūr, vol. 6, p. 47, vol. 14, pp. 163-164). It is precisely this line of reasoning—the two mentioned verses along with other similar verses—that justifies hadithologists and jurists in considering the Prophetic hadiths as an important source for discovering God's injunctions. Thus in their attempt to arrive at God's injunctions, they commonly cite Prophetic hadiths (Shāṭibī, vol. 4, p. 34; Muḥammad Sa'īd Manṣūr, p. 121; 'Abd al-Ghanī, pp. 291-308).

Shī'a and Sunnī scholars disagree as to the authoritativeness of the exegeses furnished by the Companions and the Successors. This question is closely related to another pertaining to the role of the Companions in decreeing Divine injunctions. These questions are rooted in a far earlier debate, namely, the Companions' impartiality (*'adāla*) which has been fiercely contested among scholars of uṣūl, theology, and hadith (Companions, Ṣaḥāba; Ibn Qayyim Jawziyya, vol. 4, p. 118; Shawkānī, p. 213; Ḥakīm, p. 135).

Those who advocate the imapartiality of all the Companions (Ibn Abī Ḥātam, vol. 1, p. 7; Ibn 'Abd al-Birr, vol. 1, p. 19; Ibn Athīr, vol. 1, p. 14; Ibn Ḥajar 'Asqalānī, vol. 1, p. 10) point to certain Qur'anic verses (e.g., 2:143, 3:110) and Prophetic hadiths (Ibn Munīr, vol. 2, p. 628). With this persuasion, they consider the exegeses by the Companions as an authoritative and a primary source in understanding the Qur'an.

On the other hand, the critics of this position, mainly the

Shī'a and also certain Sunnī scholars, reject the overall approval of the Companions' impartiality. They interpret differently the verses cited by the advocates and doubt the authenticity of many of the hadiths attributed to the Holy Prophet on this question (Ibn Qayyim Jawziyya, vol. 4, p. 144; Shāṭibī, vol. 4, pp. 54-55; Ḥakīm, p. 138). Certain Sunnī scholars concur with this view, thus deeming that the impartiality of a Companion, like other individuals, must be substantiated before his narration could be accepted (Āmidī, vol. 2, p. 102; 'Aḍud al-Dīn Ījī, vol. 2, p. 67). Based on this view, the exegeses of the Companions hold no special status and, at best, are equal to the inferences and opinions of other Qur'anic exegets (for further details, see Interpretation by the Companions).

Regarding the exegeses by the Prophet's Household, Sunnī and Shī'a once again diverge. Shī'as are of the conviction that the Infallible Imams hold a special status that distinguishes them as the ultimate authorities on Islamic questions and the best authorities of Qur'anic interpreters. To substantiate this, Shī'as cite a number of Qur'anic verses, e.g. 16:43(Ḥaskānī, vol. 1, p. 432; Shūshtarī, vol. 3, p. 482; Mar'ashī Najafī, vol. 14, p. 371). In addition, there are authenticated hadiths that support this position. The hadiths of *Thiqalayn* and *Ghadīr*—both of which come with numerous chains of transmission that secure them as indubitable—indicate the infallibility and imamate of the twelve Shī'a Imams. Moreover, there are authentic hadiths signifying a reciprocal relation between the Qur'an and Imam 'Alī (Shūshtarī, vol. 5, p. 639) as well as hadiths pointing to a correlation between the Qur'an and the Prophet's Household (Shūshtarī, vol. 5, p. 41; Mar'ashī Najafī, vol. 20, p. 361).

An exhaustive study of the hadiths from the Holy Prophet proves that in addition to the general exposition offered by the Holy Prophet to the Muslim community, he also provided a special exposition to the Companions and, specifically, to Imam 'Alī (Tirmidhī, vol. 6, p. 85; Kulaynī, vol. 1, p. 64; Ibn Shu'ba, p. 196; Ibn Bābiwayh, p. 257; Mizzī, vol. 7, p. 415; Majlisī, vol. 2, p.

230). Moreover, the Holy Prophet made a vital contribution to his Household to interpret the Qur'an, especially in the context of Hadith *Thiqalayn*, binding the timelessness of the Qur'an with its interpretation. As such, the exegetic hadiths narrated from the Imams, when shown to be authentic, are on a par with Prophetic hadiths as authoritative source for understanding the verses of the Qur'an. In this light, the Shī'a School holds that the statements by the Imams succeeding the Holy Prophet, expressing and interpreting the meaning of Qur'anic expressions, are in addition to the statements by the Holy Prophet himself and subsumed by the *sunna* and are thus authoritative.

Another topic concerning transmitted interpretation is the status of the exegetic hadiths. Generally speaking, exegetic hadiths are indisputably authoritative based on two conditions: when they are narrated through various chains of transmission (*mutawātir*) or otherwise, when they are reported through a single narrator (*khabar wāḥid*) but with chains of transmission that hold definitive evidence verifying their authenticity. There is little to add concerning these two categories. It is the hadiths whose issuance (*ṣudūr*), signification (*dalāla*), or circumstance (*jiha)* are uncertain that deserve detailed discussions.

Theologians and scholars of the science of principles of jurisprudence (*uṣūlīyyūn*) have long rejected the authenticity of such hadiths as far as doctrinal questions are concerned. Such questions may be resolved only where there is certainty, while these hadiths fall short of providing certainty (Khaṭīb Baghdādī, p. 472; Anṣārī, p. 109; Muḥaqqiq Ḥillī, p. 187; Ṭabāṭabā'ī, vol. 10, p. 351). Furthermore, the discussion on the authenticity of reports with single narrators is pertinent only within the province of practical injunctions as when deciding on whether or not to take an action, the believer is bound to make a choice. When there is no definitive instruction, he must resort to other options, the best and most productive being reports with a single narrator (*khabar wāḥid*). Nevertheless, it must be borne in mind that one of the strongest arguments for the authenticity of reports with single narrators the universal practice of rational people (*sīrat al-ʿuqalāʾ*; Khuʾī, p. 398). Based on this argument, one may extend the province of such reports to include doctrinal questions such as those on Qurʾanic interpretation (ibid., p. 399).

Other outstanding issues relating to transmitted interpretation are the following: weakness in the chains of transmission, the problem of fabrication, and the traditions of biblical origin (*isrāʾīliyyāt*). Although we may not entirely agree with Aḥmad ibn Ḥanbal in discounting all the reports that appear in accounts of early battles of Islam (*maghāzī*), epic poetry (*malāḥim*), and Qurʾanic interpretation (Zarkashī, vol. 2, p. 156), it must be conceded that exegetic hadiths suffer from weak chains of transmission—a problem that has been taken up by a number of scholars of Qurʾanic exegesis (e.g. Maʿrifat, vol. 2, p. 33).

Fabrication of hadiths—which was perpetrated for various motives and reasons, such as corroborating or undermining a point of view or promoting or demoting the status of a Companion—is another problem beleaguering the corpus of Qurʾanic exegesis as mentioned by Maʿrifat (vol. 2, pp. 35-56) and Dhahabī (1409/1988, vol. 1, pp. 159-165). One clear example is the fabrication of a hadith on the occasion of revelation of 9:113. Based on this fabrication, the verse implicates Abū Ṭālib, and thereby implying that he did not embrace Islam and died an infidel (Bukhārī Juʿfī, vol. 5, p. 208; Ṭabarī, vol. 7, p. 30). This verse was revealed in 9/630 while Abū Ṭālib died 618. Therefore, it would not be plausible to associate the revelation of this verse to the death of Abū Ṭālib.

Isrāʾīliyyāt—a term employed to denote reports pertaining to doctrine and Qurʾanic exegesis that have entered the Islamic corpus mainly from transmitters of Jewish origin (Dhahabī (1405/1984), p. 19)—also figure prominently in transmitted exegeses (*Isrāʾīliyyāt*). Very few exegets have succeeded in remaining unaffected by these reports (Dhahabī, 1405/1984, pp. 119-197; Abū Shuhba, pp. 260, 265, 271; Maʿrifat, vol. 2, pp. 79-311; for an example of such reports, see Rabīʿ, 1422/2001).

But in any case, historically speaking, transmitted exegesis is among the oldest methods of Qur'anic exegesis preserved in writing. A list of Shī'a transmitted exegeses includes the following: *Tafsīr Imām Ḥasan 'Askarī, Tafsīr 'Alī ibn Ibrāhīm Qummī, Tafsīr 'Ayyāshī*, and *Tafsīr Furāt Kūfī* from the earlier periods and *al-Burhān fī Tafsīr al-Qur'an* by Hāshim ibn Sulaymān al-Baḥrānī, *Tafsīr Nūr al-Thiqalayn* by 'Abd 'Alī ibn Jum'a Ḥuwayzī, and *Tafsīr Kanz al-Daqā'iq wa Baḥr al-Gharā'ib* by Muḥammad Riḍā Mashhadī Qummī, which have been written in the last few centuries.

From among the Sunnī exegeses with this orientation, one may name *Tafsīr al-Qur'an al-'Aẓīm Musnadan 'an Rasūl Allāh wa al-Ṣaḥāba wa al-Tābi'īn* by 'Abd al-Raḥmān ibn Muḥammad ibn Idrīs Rāzī, otherwise known as Ibn Abī Ḥatam Rāzī, *Tafsīr al-Qur'an al-'Aẓīm* by 'Imād al-Dīn Ismā'īl ibn 'Umar, otherwise known as Ibn Kathīr, and *al-Durr al-Manthūr fī al-Tafsīr bi al-Ma'thūr* by Jalāl al-Dīn Suyūṭī.

Some sources add the following to the above list: *Jāmi' al-Bayān 'an Ta'wīl Āyī al-Qur'an* by Muḥammad ibn Jarīr al-Ṭabarī, *al-Muḥarrar al-Wajīz fī Tafsīr al-Kitāb al-'Azīz* by Ibn 'Aṭiyya, *al-Kashf wa al-Bayān 'an Tafsīr al-Qur'an* by Abū Isḥāq Aḥmad ibn Muḥammad Tha'ālibī, *al-Jawāhir al-Ḥisān* by 'Abd al-Raḥmān ibn Muḥammad Tha'ālibī), *Baḥr al-'Ulūm* by 'Alī ibn Yaḥyā Samarqandī, Baghawī Farrā''s *Ma'ālim al-Tanzīl* (Ma'rifat, vol. 2, pp. 312-346; Dhahabī, 1409/1989, vol. 1, pp. 201-245). But considering the precise definition of transmitted interpretation, it may be judged that none of the latter titles can be characterised as such. *Ṭabarī's exegesis*, though composed largely of reports from the Holy Prophet, the Companions, and the Successors, nevertheless incorporates personal inference and analysis of the reports as well.

7. LITERARY EXEGESIS OF THE QUR'AN

Bāqir Qurbānī Zarrīn

The literary exegesis examines the Qur'an with regard to linguistic and literary aspects relating to vocabulary, syntax, and rhetoric. Many scholars and authors working in the domain of Qur'anic sciences have maintained that a Qur'anic exeget must be fully acquainted with Arabic lexicology, morphology, syntax, philology, and rhetoric (Zamakhsharī, vol. 1, p. *nūn*; Zarkashī, vol. 2, pp. 168, 173-174; Kāfiyajī, pp. 10-11; Tahānawī, vol. 1, pp. 25-26). Ibn Khaldūn (d. 808/1405; vol. 1, Introduction pp. 554-555) classifies Qur'anic exegeses into two genres: *riwā'ī* exegeses (based on hadiths and transmitted reports) and literary exegeses. Lexical exegesis is a prominent form of literary exegesis.

In the exegetic hadiths reported from the Holy Prophet and the Imams, there are cases dealing with the meanings and interpretations of certain words of the Qur'an (e.g. 'Ayyāshī, vol. 3, pp. 48, 84; Ibn Bābiwayh, p. 188; Ḥākim Nayshābūrī, vol. 2, pp. 436, 464).

'Abd Allāh ibn 'Abbās (d. 68/687) was the first exeget to offer definitions for the words in the Qur'an. To prove his point, he would cite original Arabic poetry (Ibn Sa'd, vol. 2, Part 2, p. 121). As such, he is considered the founder of this genre of Qur'anic exegesis (Sezgin, vol. 1, part one, pp. 59-61, 63-64; Kaḥḥāla, p. 62; Dhahabī, vol. 1, pp. 74-76). It is reported that he would say that for understanding obscure words of the Qur'an, one must consult Arabic poetry, for poetry is the compendium of Arab culture (*dīwān*; Suyūṭī, 1363 AHS/1983, vol. 2, p. 67). In his replies to Nāfi' ibn Azraq's questions concerning some obscure words in the Qur'an, Ibn 'Abbās quoted Arabic verse (Mubarrad, 1339/1919, vol. 3, pp. 130-132; Suyūṭī, 1363 AHS/1983, vol. 2, pp. 68-105; Goldziher, Arab. tr., p. 90; for further details on Ibn 'Abbās' works, see Sezgin, vol. 1, part 1, pp. 59-60, 66-68; Dhahabī, vol. 1, pp. 81-83; Āqā Buzurg Ṭihrānī, vol. 4, pp. 243-244). A number of works treating of Qur'anic lexicon are attributed to Ibn 'Abbās. These works are largely devoted to the exposition of certain Qur'anic words and/or their exegetic significance (Ibn 'Abbās' Qur'anic Exegesis).

'Abd Allāh ibn 'Aṭiyya (d. 383/993) is another exeget distinguished for his citation of Arabic literature by way of understanding the Qur'an, but only very few fragments of his work still survive (Sezgin, vol. 1, part 1, pp. 104-105).

Ibn Anbārī approves of the grammarians' method and discredits the position of their detractors by pointing to the practice of the Companions and the Successors in citing Arabic literature for clarifying the obscurities of the Qur'an (Quṭrubī, vol. 1, part 1, p. 24). But there was also opposition to citing Arabic literature, the argument being that the Qur'an is the guide for all things hence its self-sufficiency (Niẓām al-A'raj, vol. 1, p. 6; Suyūṭī, 1363 AHS/1984, vol. 2, p. 67).

Ibn 'Abbās' method was taken up and developed by such students of his as Mujāhid ibn Jabr, 'Ikrima, Sa'īd ibn Jubayr, Qatāda ibn Di'āma, and Ḍaḥḥāk ibn Muzāḥim (Sezgin, vol. 1, part 1, p. 65). Studies on the lexicon of the Qur'an continued into the second/eighth century. *Gharīb al-Qur'an*, i.e., obscurities in the Qur'an, *ma'ānī al-Qur'an*, i.e., meaning in the Qur'an, *mushkil al-Qur'an*, i.e., difficulties in the Qur'an, and *majāz al-Qur'an*, i.e., metaphors in the Qur'an, were titles commonly employed to denote such studies (ibid., p. 83). Early authorities treated of these titles as synonymous (Ibn Qutayba, 1378/1958, Introduction (p. III). Ibn Nadīm (Pers. tr., p. 37) describes the exegesis by Mufaḍḍal ibn Salama (d. c. 290/902) in these words: illumination for the hearts on the meaning of the Qur'an, its obscurities, and its difficulties (*ḍīyā' al-qulūb min ma'ānī al-Qur'an wa gharībih wa mushkilih*).

In their definitions, certain lexicographers cited Qur'anic verses and, in addition to treating of the lexicon, also examined grammatical issues as well as the Qur'anic recitations (*qirā'āt*; e.g. Farāhīdī, vol. 8, pp. 208, 397-398; Ṣāḥib ibn 'Abbād, vol. 7, p. 89). (The exegetic viewpoints of Khalīl ibn Aḥmad Farāhīdī have been collected from his dictionary, *al-'Ayn*, and published as an independent work under the title *Bawākīr al-Tafsīr al-Qur'anī 'ind al-Khalīl ibn Aḥmad al-Farāhīdī*.)

Various works were written during the second/eighth century on the Qur'anic lexicon, chiefly *al-Lughāt fī al-Qur'an* by Muqātil ibn Sulaymān (d. 150/767; Sezgin, vol. 1, part 1, p. 86) and the lexical exegeses by Ibn Aslam (d. 182/798) on which Ṭabarī drew in writing his own Qur'anic exegesis (ibid., p. 88). In his exegesis on certain words of the Qur'an, Ḥakīm Tirmidhī (d. 320/932) introduced the theory that though a word might be used to designate more than one meaning, all its meanings could be traced back to one original meaning from which all the others evolved (e.g. *Ḥakīm* Tirmidhī, pp. 19-24). He examines the meaning of eighty one words from the Qur'an, citing Qur'anic verses (e.g. pp. 30, 33) and, occasionally, Prophetic hadiths (e.g. pp. 36, 93-94) to expound the various meanings of a word.

In later centuries, a number of works carrying titles such as *lughāt al-Qur'an*, the lexicon of the Qur'an, were produced (for further details on such works, see Ibn Nadīm, Pers. tr., pp.

38-41; Āqā Buzurg Ṭihrānī, vol. 18, pp. 330-331). Abū Ḥayyān Gharnāṭī (d. 745/1344) classifies the Qur'anic vocabulary into two categories: one category consisting of words that even non-Arab readers acquainted with Arabic can understand and the other comprises words that only the very erudite of Arabs can comprehend. Works carrying the title of *Gharīb al-Qur'an* were written to cater to the latter group of readers (Abū Ḥayyān Gharnāṭī (1397/1976, pp. 27-28). 'Abd al-Qāhir Jurjānī (d. 471 or 474/1078 or 1081) believes (p. 303) that a study of these books shows that the number of obscure words in the Qur'an is very limited and that their obscurity arises mainly from their symbolic significance rather than from an inherent ambiguity.

The first author of a work entitled *Gharīb al-Qur'an* is Abān ibn Taghlib (d. 141/758), a Shī'a (Sezgin, vol. 1, part 1, p. 62; Ziriklī, vol. 1, pp. 26-27). Zayd ibn 'Alī ibn Ḥusayn (d. 121/738) purportedly wrote a book entitled *Tafsīr Gharīb al-Qur'an*, though it is said to have included more than just lexical discussions (Sezgin, vol. 1, part 1, p. 62; Ziriklī, vol. 1, pp. 26-27). Another work with this title was penned by Abū Fayd Mu'arrij Sadawsī (d. 195/810), a pupil of Khalīl ibn Aḥmad (Khaṭīb Baghdādī, vol. 13, p. 258; Ziriklī, vol. 7, p. 318).

Among the most esteemed authors of a *Gharīb al-Qur'an* is Ibn Qutayba (d. 276/889), whose work served as a major source for subsequent Qur'anic exegeses (Ibn Qutayba, 1378/1958), Introduction by Ṣaqr, p. IV). In this work, Ibn Qutayba first considers the etymology of the names and attributes of God in the Qur'an (pp. 6-20). Thereafter, he takes up the words that appear frequently throughout the Qur'an, such as *shirk*, *zulm*, *jinn*, and *ins* (pp. 21-37). The last part of the book is then devoted to annotations of the difficult words in the order that they appear in the Qur'an, occasionally citing Arabic poetry (pp. 42, 314) and quoting from authoritative lexicographers (p. 311).

In most other books of *gharīb al-qur'an*, words are explained alphabetically and, when necessary, by recourse to Arabic poetry (Sijistānī, pp. 153, 184) and proverbs (Abū 'Ubayd Hirawī, vol.

1, p. 223, vol. 2, pp. 146-147). In addition to elucidating the meanings of words, Rāghib Iṣfahānī (d. 502/1108), attempts to distinguish between the synonymous meanings of words (p. 6) and to bring their symbolic and metaphorical meanings to light (pp. 158, 253, 354, 390). Some of these books also discuss issues of morphology and syntax such as Abū Ḥayyān Gharnāṭī (1397/1977), pp. 46, 107, 241) and point to the non-Arabic roots of some of the words in the Qur'an (ibid., p. 226). According to Sezgin (vol. 1, part 1, pp. 61-62), Ibn 'Abbās' practice in citing Arabic poetry was entrenched as a definitive principle by the authors of *Gharīb al-Qur'an* in the second/eighth century. Moreover, many books have been written over the centuries on the topic of *gharīb al-qur'an* (Ibn Nadīm, Pers. tr., p. 37; Suyūṭī, 1408/1987), pp. 91-92; Ḥājī Khalīfa, vol. 2, col.s 1203-1204, 1207-1208; Āqā Buzurg Ṭihrānī, vol. 16, pp. 31-32, 46-50; Ganūnī, vol. 1, pp. 230-231; Zayd ibn 'Alī, Ḥusaynī Jalālī's introduction, p. 64-95; also see Gharīb al-Qur'an).

Another title used commonly for exegeses on Qur'anic lexicon is *Ma'ānī al-Qur'an*, i.e., meanings of the Qur'anic vocabulary. Ibn Ṣalāḥ (d. 643/1245) states that the term *ahl al-ma'ānī*, occasionally encountered in Qur'anic exegeses, classifies authors who have written books on *ma'ānī al-qur'an* (Ṭāshkūprīzāda, vol. 2, p. 273). One of the first scholars to write a book on this topic was Muḥammad ibn Ḥasan ibn Abī Sāra Ru'āsī Kūfī (d. 187/803), a disciple of the Imams Bāqir and Ṣādiq (AS) and a teacher of Kisā'ī and Farrā' (Dawūdī, vol. 2, p. 134; Ziriklī, vol. 6, p. 271).

Another such work was authored by Muḥammad ibn Mustanīr Quṭrub Naḥwī (d. 206/821; Ziriklī, vol. 7, p. 95), which, according to Ḥājī Khalīfa (vol. 2, col. 1730), is an unmatched and reliable source. Baghdādī (vol. 3, col. 100) indexes this book by the title *I'rāb al-Qur'an*.

Two other important works on this topic are *Ma'ānī al-Qur'an* by Yaḥyā ibn Zīyād Farrā' (d. 207/822) and *Ma'ānī al-Qur'an wa I'rābuh* by Abū Isḥāq Zajjāj (d. 311/923). These books are characterised by extensive lexical examinations (e.g. Farrā', vol. 1, pp. 114, 123; Zajjāj, vol. 1, pp. 107, 278), grammatical discussions (Farrā', vol. 1, p. 3; Zajjāj, vol. 1, p. 252), syntactical analyses of the Qur'anic recitations (*qirā'āt*; Zajjāj, vol. 1, pp. 253, 313, 384), citation of Arabic poems along with their exegesis (Farrā', vol. 1, pp. 129, 173, Zajjāj, vol. 1, pp. 254-340), quotation of proverbs (Zajjāj, vol. 1, pp. 47-48), and the various dialects considered as affecting the writing and recitation of words (Farrā', vol. 1, pp. 174, 212). Farrā's work is a lexical and grammatical study of the Qur'an, with more emphasis on the grammatical aspect. He also occasionally offers explanations on such rhetorical devices as brevity (*ījāz*), prolixity (*iṭnāb*), simile (*tashbīh*), metaphor (*istiʿāra*), and metonymy or allusion (*kināya*; Ḍayf, p. 29). Farrā' produced two other linguistic exegeses on the Qur'an as well: *al-Jamʿ wa al-Tathniya fī al-Qur'an* and *al-Maṣādir fī al-Qur'an* (Ibn Nadīm, Pers. tr., p. 73; Suyūṭī, 1384/1964), vol. 2, p. 333). In his *al-Aghfāl*, Abū ʿAlī Fārsī (d. 377/987) examines the shortcomings he perceived in the work by his teacher, Zajjāj (Āqā Buzurg Ṭihrānī, vol. 2, p. 253). (The above titles constitute only some of the books written on the topic of *maʿānī al-qur'an*; there are others not mentioned here. To learn about them, see Ibn Nadīm, Pers. tr., pp. 37, 81, 89-90, 142; Ḥājī Khalīfa, vol. 2, col. 1730; Āqā Buzurg Ṭihrānī, vol. 21, pp. 205-206.)

Another esteemed work on Qur'anic lexicon is *Majāz al-Qur'an* by Abū ʿUbayda Maʿmar ibn Muthannā (d. 210/825). Other titles such as *Gharīb al-Qur'an* and *Maʿānī al-Qur'an* attributed to this author are, according to Zabīdī and Ishbīlī, in fact other titles for the same work (Abū ʿUbayda, vol. 1, Sezgin's introduction, p. 18). It should be pointed out that in using metaphor (*majāz*), Abū ʿUbayda is mindful of the Qur'an's methods of expression rather than the technical meaning of the term as postulated in eloquent Arabic (ibid., pp. 18-19). As such, in this work, *majāz* subsumes exposition and clarification, meaning of words, morphological structure, and syntactic arrangement (Ṣāwī Juwaynī, pp. 76-77). Nevertheless,

Abū 'Ubayda's main concern is discussing the literal meaning of words by citing Arabic poetry, generally naming the poets whose works he cites (e.g. vol. 1, pp. 232, 258).

Ta'wīl Mushkil al-Qur'an by Ibn Qutayba is another prominent work of the third/ninth century, which covers a wide range of topics, such as the points of articulation, derivation, inflection (e.g. pp. 14-20), the justifications for the various recitations, polysemy (pp. 439-515), and meaningful letters (pp. 517-563). This book is distinguished by its copious citation of Arabic poetry (p. 446 and 540) and its use of the terminology from the two grammatical schools of Kūfa and Baṣra (*Ṣaqr's* introduction, p. 82). Ibn Qutayba occasionally treats of rhetorical discussions too (*Ḍayf*, p. 58).

The grammatical exegeses on the Qur'an are another form of literary exegesis. Zarkashī (d. 794/1391) asserts that an exeget must be in good command of Arabic grammar, an average understanding being insufficient (vol. 2, p. 165). Grammatical exegeses were being written as early as the second/eighth century by such scholars as Īsā ibn 'Umar Thaqafī (d. 149/766) and Abū 'Amrw Zabbān ibn 'Alā' (d. 154/770), though their works are now extinct (Sezgin, vol. 1, part 1, p. 62). Although some grammarians did not write independent works on Qur'anic exegesis, desinential inflections of Qur'anic verses figures prominently in their books on grammar (Sībawayh, vol. 5, indices, pp. 7-28; Mubarrad, 1382/1962, vol. 4, indices, pp. 229-245; Ibn Jinnī, 1372-1376/1952-1956, vol. 3, pp. 130, 256, 314; Ibn Hishām, vol. 2, pp. 531, 635). The exegetic discussions in Ibn Hishām Anṣārī's *Mughnī al-Labīb* (d. 761/1359) have also been extracted and published separately under the title of *I'rāb al-Qur'an al-Karīm min Mughnī al-Labīb*.

Parts of the book *al-Ashbāh wa al-Naẓā'ir* have been specifically written with reference to grammatical exegeses of the Qur'an. In addition, some grammarians have presented their works exclusively in connection with Qur'anic verses, basing their grammar on the Qur'anic grammar, while occasionally citing pre-Islamic poetry as well (Ḥaddād Samarqandī, pp. 368-370, 434). Major parts of books written on Qur'anic recitations are devoted to grammatical analysis, enunciating the morphological and syntactic arguments in support of one recitation or another are harmonised with Arabic poetry (e.g. Ibn Khāliwayh, 1413/1992, vol. 1, pp. 197, 225; Abū 'Alī Fārsī, vol. 1, pp. 20, 89; Ibn Jinnī, 1419/1998, vol. 1, p. 117), and the different dialects (Abū 'Alī Farsī, vol. 1, p. 86; Ibn Jinnī, 1419/1999, vol. 1, p. 137).

The books on *i'rāb al-qur'an*, i.e., the desinential inflections of Qur'anic verses, constitute the bulk of the grammatical exegeses on the Qur'an. The authors of these books take different approaches. Some, like Makkī ibn Abī Ṭālib Ḥamūsh (d. 437/1045) in the book entitled *Mushkil 'Arab al-Qur'an*, only cover the difficult verses of the Qur'an, while others, like Ibn Anbārī (d. 577/1181) in his *al-Bayān fī I'rāb Gharīb al-Qur'an*, treat of obscure verses exclusively. Still some authors examine the entire Qur'an, such as 'Ukbarī (d. 616/1219) in his *al-Tibyān fī I'rāb al-Qur'an* and *Imlā' Mā Manna bih al-Raḥmān*. Other approaches taken have been to study the recitations along with the syntactical structures or to bring together all similar syntactical functions under the same heading (e.g. *I'rāb al-Qur'an*, ascribed to Zajjāj, 'Ukbarī, part 1, Bajāwī's introduction, pp. III-IV).

Despite differences, books on *i'rāb al-qur'an* share some common features. These include:

1. Studying the origins of the words and their meanings attested in the Qur'an (e.g. Ibn Khāliwayh, 1411/1990, pp. 6-8; 'Ukbarī, Ibrāhīm 'Atwa 'Iwaḍ's edition, vol. 1, p. 206);

2. Morphological discussions (Zajjāj, 1406/1985), part 3, pp. 866-882; Ibn Anbārī, vol. 1, p. 171);

3. Citing Arabic poetry on lexical and syntactic questions (Zajjāj, 1406/1985, part 1, p. 283; 'Ukbarī Ibrāhīm 'Atwa 'Iwaḍ's edition, vol. 2, p. 10);

4. Comparing the viewpoints of the grammarians of Baṣra, Kūfa, and Baghdād (Zajjāj, 1406/1985, part 1, pp. 214, 283-284;

Makkī ibn Abī Ṭālib Ḥamūsh, part 1, p. 66);

5. Considering rhetorical topics where pertinent (Zajjāj, 1406/1985, part 1, p. 156, part 3, p. 909);

6. Examining the different recitations of a verse (Zajjāj, 1406/1985, part 1, p. 156; part 3, pp. 946-957; 'Ukbarī, Ibrāhīm 'Aṭwa 'Iwaḍ's edition, vol. 2, pp. 51, 218. To learn more about the books on *i'rāb al-qur'an*, see Ṭāshkūprīzāda, vol. 2, p. 279; Ḥājī Khalīfa, vol. 1, cols. 121-123; Āqā Buzurg Ṭihrānī, vol. 2, pp. 235-236; Zajjāj, 1406/1985, part 3, Abyārī's epilogue, p. 1092; Ganūnī, vol. 1, pp. 177-178).

The third category of literary exegeses constitute rhetorical ones. Rhetorical figures are considered as one of the constituents of the Qur'anic sciences. In order to prove the inimitability (*i'jāz*) of the Qur'an, Muslims established rhetoric as a systematic discipline, thus incorporating the main discussions into the books on the genre (the Qur'an, Inimitability). 'Abd al-Qāhir Jurjānī (p. 236) censures exegets as uninformed who are unacquainted with rhetoric and who, as a result, confuse the metaphorical and literal meanings of words. Zamakhsharī (d. 538/1143; vol. 1, p. XI) states that to discover the true meaning of the Qur'an, it is necessary to be well-versed in the two branches of rhetoric dealing with verbal expression of concepts and content and the metaphorical language (*ma'ānī* and *bayān*), and regards them as exclusively Qur'anic. Sakkākī (d. 626/1228) also criticises exegets ignorant of these two branches (p. 77), for, in his view, comprehending the subtleties and mysteries of the Qur'an is possible only for one learned in them (pp. 196-199).

Among the earliest to write in the genre of literary exegesis is Jāhiz (d. 255). He wrote a book that studied the verses of the Qur'an as regards brevity, omission, and metaphor (Jāhiz, vol. 3, p. 86). Ibn Nadīm (Pers. tr., p. 41) names several authors, including Ibn Ikhshīd (d. 326) and Abū 'Alī Ḥasan ibn 'Alī ibn Naṣr, with books entitled *Naẓm al-Qur'an*.

Some scholars of rhetoric have written their books with Abundant references to the Qur'an, e.g. Ibn Abī Iṣba' (d.

654/1256) in his *Taḥrīr al-Taḥbīr* and *Badīʿ al-Qurʾan*; see Bayān), Zarkashī (e.g. vol. 2, pp. 254-299, vol. 3, pp. 414-444), and Suyūṭī (1363 AHS/1983, vol. 3, pp. 142-165).

Sharīf Raḍī (d. 406/1015) produced the first exegesis on the Qurʾan taking Arabic rhetoric into consideration, entitled *Talkhīṣ al-Bayān fī Majāzāt al-Qurʾan*. In this book, Sharīf Raḍī classifies the metaphors and metonymys in the Qurʾan in the standard order of the chapters and verses under the general heading of *majāz*, i.e., metaphor, while also enriching his study with numerous citations of Arabic poetry (pp. 143, 169, 179; for more details, see *Talkhīṣ al-Bayān fī Majāzāt al-Qurʾan*).

In addition to the exclusively literary exegeses, mention should be made of exegeses that, though consider other issues as well, have a strong literary aspect. *Jāmiʿ al-Bayān fī Tafsīr al-Qurʾan* by Muḥammad ibn Jarīr Ṭabarī (d. 310/922) is a prime example of this category of exegeses. This work is a rich reservoir of lexical and literary comments—including Arabic poetry and various Arabic dialects—and thus is considered a credible source for lexical and grammatical discussions on the Qurʾan (e.g. Ṭabarī, vol. 1, pp. 83-84, vol. 2, pp. 12-13; in this relation, also see Ṭabarī›s Exegesis).

Remaining exegeses in this category that are worthy of note can be briefly introduced as followed;

1. Qurʾanic exegesis by Abū ʿAlī Fārsī, from which Shaykh Ṭūsī quotes in his *Tibyān* (Āqā Buzurg Ṭihrānī, vol. 4, p. 255).

2. *Al-Burhān fī Tafsīr al-Qurʾan* by ʿAlī ibn Ibrāhīm Ḥawfī (d. 430/1038). This exegesis is, according to Ḥājī Khalīfa (vol. 1, col. 241), primarily concerned with desinential inflection (*iʿrāb*) and the obscure words and phrases (*gharīb*).

3. *Al-Amālī*, alternately known as *Ghurar al-Fawāʾid wa Durar al-Qalāʾid*, by Sayyid Murtaḍā ʿAlam al-Hudā (d. 436/1044). This exegesis covers a wide range of themes, encompassing lexical, grammatical, rhetorical, and theological questions, and as such is ranked among the important works of the fifth/thirteenth century. It reflects the author's amazing memory and expertise

in poetry and the lexicon. In his lexical analyses, 'Alam al-Hudā invokes pristine Arabic lexicon and ancient Arabic poetry to corroborate a point of view (Goldziher, Arab. tr., pp. 137-139; Dhahabī, vol. 1, pp. 388-399). This work is characterised by including the following literary features: lexical discussions (vol. 1, p. 13), grammatical discussions (vol. 1, pp. 504-505), citation of ancient poetry in determining the meaning of words (vol. 1, p. 453), consideration of the various dialects (vol. 1, p. 293), and rhetorical discussions (vol. 2, pp. 71-75, 144-145, 154-155).

4. *Al-Tibyān fī Tafsīr al-Qur'an* by Abū Ja'far Ṭūsī (d. 460/1067). This work is one of the most authoritative of Shī'a exegeses on the Qur'an.

5. *Al-Basīṭ* by Wāḥidī Nayshābūrī (d. 468/1075). Ḥājī Khalīfa (vol. 1, col. 431) classifies this work as a grammatical exegesis.

6. *Kashf al-Mushkilāt* by 'Alī ibn Ḥusayn Iṣfahānī Jāmi' (fl. ca. 535/1140). Ziriklī (vol. 4, p. 279) states that this work treats of lexical and grammatical arguments for the divergent Qur'anic recitations.

7. *Al-Kashshāf 'an Ḥaqā'iq Ghawāmiḍ al-Tanzīl wa 'Uyūn al-Aqāwīl fī Wujūh al-Ta'wīl* by Maḥmūd ibn 'Umar Zamakhsharī. It is among the most comprehensive exegeses on grammar and rhetoric in the Qur'an (*al-Kashshāf 'an Ḥaqā'iq al-Tanzīl*). Ibn Khaldūn (vol. 1, introduction, pp. 555-556) praises the book as one of the best literary exegeses on the Qur'an, though objects to the author's Mu'tazilī opinions (for further details onthis and the literary value of this work, see Dhahabī, vol. 1, pp. 433-446; *Ḍayf*, pp. 243-265). Grammatical discussions are given thorough consideration in this exegesis (e.g. vol. 1, pp. 245-246; 387-388). Among the rhetorical topics Zamakhsharī deals with, one may point to simile (*tashbīh*; vol. 1, pp. 79-81). He also argues that metonymy (*kināya*) should be acknowledged as a form of metaphor (vol. 1, pp. 654-655) and elaborates on the difference between allusion (*ta'rīḍ*) and metonymy (*kināya*; vol. 1, pp. 282-283). Important topics from the three subdisciplines of Arabic rhetoric— the three branches of rhetoric dealing with verbal

expression of concepts and content, the metaphorical language, and figures of speech and the art of beautiful style (*ma'ānī, bayān, badī'*)—also find ample treatment in this work (for more detail, see Ibrāhīm 'Iṭwa 'Iwaḍ, pp. 158-189; Ḥawfī, pp. 205-231).

8. *Al-Muḥarrar al-Wajīz fī Tafsīr al-Kitāb al-'Azīz* by Ibn 'Aṭiyya Andalusī (d. 541/1146 or 546/1151). The author's focus in this work is on literary issues (Manī' 'Abd al-Ḥalīm Maḥmūd, p. 126; Dhahabī, vol. 1, p. 233). In writing his book, Ibn 'Aṭiyya consulted many lexical and grammatical sources and, as such, his exegesis is very well thought of in these two fields (Ibn 'Aṭiyya's Introduction, vol. 1, pp. 4, 8). Ibn Khaldūn claims (Introduction vol. 1, p. 555) that this exegesis was especially popular in Morocco and Andalusia and that Quṭrubī (see below) follows Ibn 'Aṭiyya's method. The major features of this book are extensive discussion of grammatical questions (e.g. vol. 1, pp. 225-226, 281), Abundant citation of Arabic poetry (e.g. vol. 1, pp. 351, 354), and grammatical examination of the recitations (vol. 1, pp. 434, 444).

9. *Majma' al-Bayān fī Tafsīr al-Qur'an* by Faḍl ibn Ḥasan Ṭabarsī (d. 548/1153). The author confidently states (vol. 1, p. 77) that his exegesis will serve as a lexical and grammatical source for others. The work is characterised by order, systematic arrangement, and coordination of subject matter. On lexical questions, Ṭabarsī offers keen insights by invoking Arabic poetry (e.g. vol. 1, p. 196). He also gives sufficient consideration to grammatical questions (e.g. vol. 1, p. 176; for further details, see Ibrāhīm 'Iṭwa 'Iwaḍ, pp. 124-125; Dhahabī, vol. 2, pp. 95-98; also see *Majma' al-Bayān fī Tafsīr al-Qur'an*).

10. *Jawāmi' al-Jāmi'* also by Faḍl ibn Ḥasan Ṭabarsī. In this work, the author is particularly concerned with Zamaksharī's exegesis (vol. 1, pp. 2-3). The author pursues lexical, grammatical, and rhetorical topics (vol. 1, pp. 9, 249, 340), investigating the views of grammarians of Kūfa and Baṣra (e.g. vol. 1, p. 15), while also deploying popular proverbs (vol. 1, pp. 23, 207).

11. *Mafātīḥ al-Asrār wa Maṣābīḥ al-Abrār* by Muḥammad ibn

'Abd al-Karīm Shahristānī (d. 548/1153). In this work, after each verse the author dwells on questions relating to lexicon and meaning (e.g. vol. 1, p. 243) and grammar (vol. 1, p. 228) with reference to Arabic poetry (vol. 1, pp. 219, 229). In the opening to his exegesis (vol 1, pp. 172-174), the author enumerates the lexicographers, grammarians, and exegets from whose work he has benefitted— Farrā', Zajjāj, Kisā'ī, Ibn Sallām, Abū 'Ubayda, and Quṭrub.

12. *Al-Tafsīr al-Kabīr* (known as *Mafātīḥ al-Ghayb*) by Fakhr Rāzī (d. 606/1209; *Tafsīr Kabīr*). Some of the literary features of this exegesis are as follows: in depth lexical examination with recourse to Arabic literature (Fakhr Rāzī, vol. 1, pp. 156-164, vol. 2, pp. 12-13, 68), treatment of grammatical and rhetorical discussions (vol. 1, pp. 96-100, vol. 2, pp. 72, 74-75; for a thorough discussion of rhetoric in Fakh Rāzī's exegesis, see Māhir Mahdī Hilāl, pp. 187-255).

13. *Al-Jāmi' li-Aḥkām al-Qur'an* by Muḥammad ibn Aḥmad Anṣārī Quṭrubī (d. 671/1272). Though this work is more known for its jurisprudential (*fiqhī*) exegeses, it also encompasses noteworthy literary discussions, including lexical analyses and grammatical and rhetorical studies (e.g. Quṭrubī, vol. 1, part 1, pp. 136-138, 210-211, part 2, pp. 239-241; see also Quṭrubī's Exegesis).

14. *Anwār al-Tanzīl wa Asrār al-Ta'wīl* by 'Abd Allāh ibn 'Umar Bayḍāwī (d. 685/1286 or 691/1291). A discussion of grammar and lexicon (e.g. vol. 1, pp. 15, 66, 103), frequently citing Arabic poetry (e.g. vol. 1, pp. 18, 137), pointing out the grammatical differences between the two schools of Baṣra and Kūfa (e.g. vol. 1, p. 83), and grammatically analysing the divergent recitations (e.g. vol. 1, pp. 121, 123) are among the literary features of this exegesis (Bayḍāwī, 'Abd Allāh ibn 'Umar).

15. *Madārik al-Tanzīl wa Ḥaqā'iq al-Ta'wīl* by 'Abd Allāh ibn Aḥmad Nasafī (d. 701/1301 or 710/1310). This exegesis is essentially a recapitulation of the exegeses by Zamakhsharī and Bayḍāwī while augmenting them with grammatical analysis, quotations from grammarians, and a tendency to underscore the rhetorical perfections in the Qur'an (e.g. Nasafī, vol. 1, pp. 5,

23, 386, 565; also see Jubūrī, part 1, p. 114, Ṣāliḥ, p. 293).

16. *Gharā'ib al-Qur'an wa Raghā'ib al-Furqān* by Niẓām al-Dīn A'raj Nayshābūrī (d. 728/1327). The author states (vol. 1, pp. 6-7) that his purpose in this work is to resolve the problems of Zamkhsharī's *Kashshāf*, while also explaining the words in the Qur'an, its metonymies, and metaphors. He ends his exegesis (vol. 6, p. 606) by listing his sources, and among his literary sources he names Jawharī's *al-Ṣiḥāḥ*, Zamakhsharī's *al-Kashshāf*, Fakhr Rāzī's *Tafsīr Kabīr*, and Sakkākī's *al-Miftāḥ* (*Miftāḥ al-'Ulūm*).

17. *Al-Baḥr al-Muḥīṭ* by Abū Ḥayyān Gharnāṭī (d. 745/1344). The author professes (vol. 1, pp. 3-5) to have revealed in this exegesis the subtleties of the branch of rhetoric dealing with metaphorical language (*bayān*) and the intricate grammatical points and to have enriched his lexical and grammatical studies by separately considering the issues relating to the disciplines of metaphorical language and figurative devices (*bayān* and *badī'*). Gharnāṭī acknowledges the exegeses by Zamakhsharī and Ibn 'Aṭiyya as his sources (vol. 1, pp. 9-11). His treatment of matters of morphology (vol. 1, p. 23) and syntax (vol. 1, pp. 191-192) are so extensive that some scholars have viewed his work as more akin to grammatical books than to Qur'anic exegeses (Dhahabī, vol. 1, p. 301). The author extends his study to encompass rhetorical discussions of the Qur'an as well (vol. 1, pp. 50-51, 186). He also makes frequent references to Arabic poetry (vol. 1, pp. 172, 202). The author later wrote a concise version of this exegesis and named it *al-Nahr al-Mādd min al-Baḥr* (Ḥājī Khalīfa, vol. 1, col. 226).

18. *Tafsīr al-Qur'an* by Aḥmad ibn Yūsuf Samīn Ḥalabī (d. 756/1355). According to Ḥājī Khalīfa (vol. 1, col. 122) this exegesis is an outstanding work in its treatment of the five disciplines of grammar, morphology, lexicon, verbal expression of concepts and content (*ma'ānī*), and metaphorical language (*bayān*). Some scholars, however, disagree, criticising the exegesis for including redundancy and prolixity. The author has also written books on Qur'anic grammar and Qur'anic obscurities (Ziriklī, vol. 1, p. 274).

19. *Tafsīr al-Qur'an al-'Aẓīm* by Ibn Kathīr Damishqī (d.

774/1372). In addition to considering discussions on lexicon, grammar, and rhetoric in the Qur'an, this work lays great emphasis on Arabic poetry. The author's aims in laying emphasis on Arabic poetry may be classified into three groups:

1. Citing poetry to better understand the meaning of words (e.g. vol. 1, pp. 88, 277-278),

2. Using the historical incidents mentioned in prestigious poems to interpret the Qur'an and to clarify historical questions (vol. 1, pp. 255, 499-500),

3. Pointing to the poetry inspired by Qur'anic passages (e.g. vol. 1, pp. 471-498), thus illustrating the influence of the Qur'an on Arabic poetry.

20. *Baṣā'ir Dhawī al-Tamyīz fī Laṭā'if al-Kitāb al-'Azīz* by Majd al-Dīn Muḥammad ibn Ya'qūb Fīrūzābādī. The author elucidates various points in alphabetical order, separating each point with the heading *baṣīra*. He starts each heading by treating literary discussions pertinent to the letter in question. For instance, he analyses the letter *alif* from grammatical, morphological, and philological perspectives, citing poetry as evidence (vol. 2, pp. 4-11), and in this manner he offers valuable insights. In discussing grammatical issues, the author points to the etymology of words, their meanings, and usages (vol. 2, pp. 113-114). His treatment of grammatical matters is based on their application in the Qur'an (vol. 2, pp. 190-195).

21. *Irshād al-'Aql al-Salīm ilā Mazāyā al-Qur'an al-Karīm* by Abū al-Su'ūd Muḥammad 'Imādī (d. 982/1574). The author considers the various aspects of the Qur'anic inimitability with a rhetorical approach (Ṣāliḥ, p. 293). This exegesis holds an especially prominent position, such that it is considered by some as the most important exegesis next to Zamakhsharī and Bayḍāwī's (Dhahabī, vol. 1, pp. 328-329). In addition to rhetorical issues though, Abū al-Su'ūd also discusses morphological and grammatical questions with recourse to Arabic poetry (e.g. vol. 1, pp. 10, 15, 24, 174).

22. *Rūḥ al-Bayān* by Ismā'īl Ḥaqqī (d. 1137/1724). This exegesis

is primarily in the Sufi tradition but it does also contains lexical and rhetorical exposition, occasionally interposing Persian and Turkish passages into the main Arabic body (Mani' 'Abd al-Halīm Maḥmūd, pp. 267-268). The author frequently quotes Persian poetry with the names of the poets (vol. 1, pp. 3 and 252 for his quotations from Rumi; vol. 1, p. 6 for quotations from Ḥāfiẓ and Sa'dī; vol. 1, p. 192 for quotations from Amīr Khusruw Dihlawī).

23. *Fatḥ al-Qadīr al-Jāmi' bayn Fannay al-Riwāya wa al-Dirāya min 'Ilm al-Tafsīr* by Muḥammad ibn 'Alī Shawkānī (d. 1250/1834). The author asserts (vol. 1, p. 13) that in the exegesis he leans mainly toward lexical, grammatical, and rhetorical issues. He quotes abundantly from such lexicographers as Ibn Fāris and Azharī Hirawī (e.g. vol. 1, pp. 33, 97) but is at the same time attentive to grammar and rhetoric, for which he cites Arabic poetry (e.g. vol. 1, pp. 45, 52, 208).

24. *Rūḥ al-Ma'ānī fī Tafsīr al-Qur'an al-'Aẓīm wa al-Sab' al-Mathānī* by Maḥmūd Ālūsī Baghdādī (d. 1270/1853). His attention to grammatical matters is so exaggerated that it distracts his function as an exeget (Dhahabī, vol. 1, p. 338). Some of the features of this exegesis are the author's extensive dwelling on grammatical issues (e.g. vol. 1, pp. 232-233, vol. 2, pp. 87-88), frequent citation of Arabic poetry (e.g. vol. 1, pp. 282-361), and treatment of rhetorical questions (e.g. vol. 1, pp. 160-163).

8. JURISPRUDENTIAL EXEGESIS OF THE QUR'AN

Mihrdād ʿAbbāsī

The exegetic approach that focuses on, categorises, and analyses Qur'anic verses related to religious injunctions is denominated as jurisprudential (*fiqhī*) exegesis. The two disciplines of Qur'anic exegesis and jurisprudence developed undoubtedly within the same historical course (Shihābī, vol. 1, p. 478). Thus they are connected in their principles, methods of understanding, and resources, since in Islamic doctrine, the primary source for deriving religious injunctions is the Qur'an. Maʿrifat believes (vol. 2, p. 354, n. 1) that taking political and social aspects into account, to which former scholars were largely indifferent, the number of injunctive or prescriptive verses (*āyāt fiqhī*) may exceed as many as two thousand. The generally accepted view in the Shīʿa school, however, holds this number at five hundred (e.g. ʿAllāma Ḥillī, vol. 1, p. 526; Fāḍil Miqdād, vol. 1, p. 5; Shahīd Thānī, vol. 3, pp. 63-64; Bahrānī, vol. 1, p. 27). These verses, which ordain the injunctions and practical duties of Muslims, cover a variety of issues—e.g., domestic, social, and economic (for further details on the classification of the injunctive verses, see Mas'ūdī, pp. 55-61).

The Qur'an commonly enunciates its injunctions in general terms. In many cases, injunctions are expressed in terms whose denotation is not definitive and obvious, leaving the way open to personal opinion and speculation. Furthermore, differences of opinion on lexical, grammatical, and legal issues—such as the general and the particular (*'umūm wa khuṣūṣ*), the absolute and the qualified (*iṭlāq wa taqyīd*)—and on the question of the authenticity and the degree of a hadith's credibility may lead to disagreement among exegets and jurisprudents in extracting an injunction from the Qur'an (Āl Ja'far, p. 157; Rūmī, vol. 2, p. 416; for instances of such disagreements, see Āl Ja'far, pp. 232-255). Such disagreements appeared immediately after the Holy Prophet's demise among the Companions as to the meaning of a particular verse and the injunctions derivable there from (e.g. Khiḍrī, pp. 97-105; Dhahabī, vol. 2, p. 415). These disagreements persisted till the formation of the official jurisprudential schools, and further complicated by the introduction of new questions into the Islamic community. The founders of the schools responded by offering various arguments in support of what they deemed correct, while trying to stay clear of personal bias.

Following this period, the trendency toward adoption of the legal decision of a school of law (*taqlīd*) came into existence. In the course of this move, the adherents of the various schools were motivated by the purpose of proving the opinions of their respective authorities and disproving those of opposing schools. In so doing, they resorted to offering interpretations for verses contradicting their apparent meanings (*ta'wīl*), declaring verses rescinded by hadith or other verses (*naskh*), and considering verses qualified by hadith or other verses (*takhṣīṣ*) to demonstrate that Qur'anic verses buttressed respective jurisprudential views or, at least, did not contradict them (Dhahabī, vol. 2, pp. 414-417). In addition to the formation of the jurisprudential schools, the second/eighth and third/ninth centuries thus witnessed the systematic formation of jurisprudential exegesis based on the respective schools (Ayāzī, pp. 89-90).

Subsequently, the adherents of each school would formulate injunctions based on their distinctive principles by deriving injunctions from Qur'anic verses and writing exegeses on injunctive verses clearly reflecting sectarian differences. In such works, the author usually began by stating the views of the jurisprudents and authorities of the rival schools along with their arguments. They then went on to show the superiority of their own view, which invariably corresponded to their respective jurisprudential school, with recourse to lexical, grammatical, and jurisprudential points, further supplementing cases with citations from the Qur'an and hadith. In this connection, it may be appropriate to cite verse six, sura al-Mā'ida (minor ritual ablution, i.e. āya al-wuḍū) which subsumes numerous practical rules (Ibn 'Arabī, part 2, pp. 557-558). Diverging grammatical and jurisprudential arguments as well as the various possibilities as to the meaning of the conjunction "and" (*wāw*) have led to many disagreements. These have resulted in views that declare observing the specified order as obligatory in the minor ritual ablution and those that deny the necessity of observing the specified order (Jaṣṣāṣ, vol. 2, pp. 360-364; Ibn 'Arabī, part 2, pp. 561-562; Quṭrubī, vol. 3, section 6, pp. 98-99; Fāḍil Miqdād, vol. 1, pp. 19-22).

Jurisprudential exegesis is concerned exclusively with rules pertained to legal capacity (*taklīfī*) and convention (*waḍ'ī*; Ma'rifat, vol. 2, p. 354). In this approach, the exeget strives to infer injunctions from Qur'anic verses that contain a religious injunction explicitly or implicitly (Ayāzī, p. 88). As such, jurisprudential exegesis may be catalogued among the earliest of thematic exegeses. As it is taken up mainly by jurisprudents, it is considered as one of the most stringent approaches to Qur'anic exegesis (Ma'rifat's introduction to Anṣārī, p. 9). In treating a prescriptive verse, jurisprudential exegeses elucidate all issues related to the injunction in question. This is to such an extent as to compel Rūmī to state (vol. 2, p. 417) that there is not much of a difference between such exegeses and standard jurisprudential texts, whereas in other methods of Qur'anic exegesis, the exeget confines himself to explaining the injunction explicitly mentioned in the verse and his exposition of it (for further details, see Āl Ja'far, p. 146).

Jurisprudential exegets generally pursue one of two ways in their exegeses: 1. taking on the prescriptive verses in the order according to which they appear in the Qur'an or 2. classifying the prescriptive verses according to the standard order of jurisprudential texts. Sunnī jurisprudents generally follow the first method whereas Shī'as take the second (Ayāzī, pp. 90-91; Mudīrshānihchī, p. 5).

The prescriptive hadiths from the Prophet and their exposition by the Companions and the Prophet's Household are included in jurisprudential exegeses (Ma'rifat, vol. 2, p. 355), although, according to Dhahabī (vol. 2, p. 418), prior to the Period of Compilation (*'aṣr tadwīn*), there were no jurisprudential exegeses save fragmentary statements by the Companions and the Successors. Ibn Nadīm (Pers. tr., pp. 40-41) names Muḥammad ibn Sā'ib Kalbī (d. 146/763), a disciple of the Imams Bāqir and Ṣādiq (AS), as among the authors of jurisprudential exegeses. Based on this, Sayyid Ḥasan Ṣadr (p. 321) considers him the earliest author to pen an exegesis on the prescriptive verses of the Qur'an. The work, however, is now lost.

The earliest jurisprudential exegesis extant was authored by Muḥammad ibn Idrīs Shāfi'ī (d. 204/819) and compiled by Aḥmad ibn Ḥusayn Bayhaqī (d. 458/1065). Abū Bakr Aḥmad ibn 'Alī Jaṣṣāṣ (d. 370/980), affiliated with the Ḥanafī school, was the next to write such an exegesis. Thereafter, writing jurisprudential exegeses became common practice (Ma'rifat's introduction to Anṣārī, pp. 9-10). Various scholars wrote exegeses on this theme, including Abū al-Ḥasan 'Alī ibn Muḥammad Kīyāharāsī (d. 504/1110-1111) from the Shāfi'ī school, Abū Bakr Muḥammad ibn 'Abd Allāh ibn 'Arabī (d. 543/1148-1149), and Abū 'Abd Allāh Muḥammad ibn Aḥmad Quṭrubī (d. 671/1272-1273) from the Mālikī school, and Muḥammad ibn Ḥusayn ibn Qāsim (d. 1067/1656-1657) from the Zaydī school (Dhahabī, vol. 2, pp. 418-419). *Zād al-Masīr fī 'Ilm al-Tafsīr* by Ibn Jawzī (d. 597/1200-1201), though not confined to the prescriptive verses, is largely based on the jurisprudential views of the Ḥanbalī school (Ibn Jawzī, p. 72; Dhahabī, vol. 2, pp. 414-420, ignoring the jurisprudential exegeses by Ḥanbalī scholars; Rūmī, vol. 2, p. 417; for further details on jurisprudential exegeses by Sunnī scholars, see Ḥājī Khalīfa, vol. 1, col. 20; Ayāzī, p. 837).

In the Imāmī school, the earliest work devoted entirely to jurisprudential exegesis is by Quṭb al-Dīn Abū al-Husayn Sa'īd ibn Hiba Allāh Rāwandī (d. 573/1177-1178; Ma'rifat's introduction to Anṣārī, p. 10). Fāḍil Miqdād Suyūrī (d. 826/1422-1423) was the next Shī'a scholar to write such an exegesis, acknowledged as an exhaustive work in its own right (for further details on jurisprudential exegeses in the Shī'a school, see Āqā Buzurg Ṭihrānī, vol. 1, pp. 40-44; Ayāzī, pp. 91-92).

Recent works in the genre of jurisprudential exegesis are few and are markedly different from their earlier predecessors. The most important features of recent jurisprudential exegeses are as follows: 1. discussing only the general and important topics and avoiding prolixity 2. staying aloof from sectarian concerns and rising above a particular jurisprudential school; 3. making a point of replying to critiques leveled at such injunctions as severing the hand of thieves and stoning adulterers; 4. dwelling only on some of the descriptive verses as these are texts written mainly for the benefit of seminary students studying Qur'anic sciences (Rūmī, vol. 2, pp. 418-419, 436; Mudīrshānihchī, pp. 3-4).

A current trend today is to compile the views of a renowned historic personage without an independent exegesis on the prescriptive verses scattered throughout his works on Qur'anic exegesis or jurisprudence and to publish them as one work. Products of these include *al-Aḥkām al-Fiqhiyya li-*

'l-Imām al-Ṭabarī: Majmūʿa min Kitāb al-Tafsīr lahū (Beirut: 2000) compiled by Muḥammad Ḥasan Ismāʿīl and organised according to the standard order of jurisprudential texts, and *al-Anẓār al-Tafsīriyya li-'l-Shaykh al-Anṣārī* (Qum: 1376 AHS/1998) compiled by Ṣāḥibʿalī Muḥibbī and organised according the order of Qur'anic suras (to learn more on the works published on jurisprudential exegesis, see Hāshimzādih, pp. 169-184).

9. RATIONAL- THEOLOGICAL EXEGESIS OF THE QUR'AN

Muḥsin Mu'īnī

In the rational-theological approach, rather than invoking hadiths, the exeget relies on his own judgment and deduction in understanding the verses of the Qur'an while resorting to the disciplines of theology and philosophy to, occasionally, substantiate his own theological views or refute those of his opponents. In the discipline of Qur'anic exegesis, this genre is designated as extrapolative (*ijtihādī*) or subjective (*bi al-ra'y*) exegesis (Muḥammad Ḥusayn Dhahabī, vol. 1, p. 256; Zurqānī, vol. 2, p. 49; Ayāzī, 1414/1994, p. 40).

The emergence and development of rational-theological exegeses was encouraged in large part by the numerous verses in the Qur'an encompassing rational and speculative propositions, such as those promoting intellectual reflection (e.g. Qur'an 2:242, 21:67, 23:80, 24:61) or those with a rationalistic tone (e.g. the verses refuting polytheism; see Qur'an 21:22, 27:63). In addition, the Qur'an contains verses whose interpretation and exposition would be impossible if one were to take them at face value and without recourse to rational interpretation, especially verses that appear to be in conflict with the explicit tenets of the Qur'an itself. Verses in which God is anthropomorphically described as having a hand or a face (48:10, 2:115, 55:27) or resting on His throne (20:5) or as being seen (75:22-23) are of this category. These verses, which are linked to such theological concepts as anthropomorphism (*tashbīh*) and deanthropomorphism (*tanzīh*), have occasioned the introduction of related theological questions.

Moreover, one occasionally encounters verses in the Qur'an that are seemingly irreconcilable. For instance, on the one hand, there are verses affirming that God guides and misleads whomever He wishes (Qur'an 14:4, 16:93, 74:31) and, on the other hand, verses exhorting humankind to shun disbelief and embrace faith (Qur'an 3:79, 7:158, 4:136). In the exegesis on these verses, various subject matters, which are in the main of a theological and philosophical nature, have been raised—such as predestination, freewill, acquisition, human action, and vice and virtue. These verses and other factors provoked discussions and disputes in the early centuries of Islam, eventually leading to the development of Islamic theology. This, in turn, had a direct influence on Qur'anic exegesis, which hitherto had remained largely based on traditions narrated from the Holy Prophet and his Companions. In comparison to transmitted exegesis, rational-theological exegesis is, at least as far as written works are concerned, of later development, though its roots have been traced back to the period of the Successors (Ma'rifat, vol. 2, p. 349; Rūmī, p. 100). In relation to this, the exegetic school of Iraq is, in opposition to those of Mecca and Medina, characterised by its extrapolative approach (Muḥammad Ḥusayn Dhahabī, vol. 1, pp. 121-122; Khuḍayrī, vol. 2, pp. 722-723).

In the third/ninth and fourth/tenth centuries, as theology advanced so did theological exegesis of the Qur'an. In relation to this, the Mu'tazilī exegeses were groundbreaking. Based on their theological school, the Mu'tazilīs pursued a rationalistic interpretation of the Qur'an, labeling verses whose apparent meaning concurred with their understanding as precise (*muḥkam*) and those that were not as equivocal (*mutashābih*). In respect to the latter, they would resort to offering an interpretation that is incongruous with the apparent meaning of a verse (*ta'wīl*; Ṣāwī Juwaynī, p. 108; for further details on the role of *ta'wīl* as perceived by the Muʿtazilīs and, particularly, the Muʿtazilī Jāḥiẓ and Qāḍī ʿAbd al-Jabbār ibn Aḥmad Hamadānī, see Ṣāwī Juwaynī, pp. 108-112, 118-297; Abū Zayd, pp. 180-239). The Muʿtazilīs were among the first to lay great emphasis on rationalism in Qur'anic exegesis. This tendency was condemned by their rivals as subjective interpretation (*tafsīr bi-'l-ra'y*), and had been denounced by the Holy Prophet in a number of hadiths (see section one: General Points).

To counter the views of the Muʿtazilī theologians, many non-Muʿtazilī theologians and exegets—e.g., Abū al-Ḥasan Ashʿarī, Māturīdī, and Fakhr Rāzī—eventually also took up a rationalistic approach in their Qur'anic exegeses, and this led to a new division. In their classification of Qur'anic exegeses, scholars of Qur'anic exegesis and Ashʿarīs later condoned these rationalist attempts as "laudable" or "permissible" subjective interpretations, as opposed to those by Muʿtazilīs and other schools which they discredited as "condemnable" subjective interpretation (Muḥammad Ḥusayn Dhahabī, vol. 1, pp. 288-289, 362-477; Zurqānī, vol. 2, pp. 65-69; Rūmī, pp. 102-104; Suyūṭī, 1363 AHS/1983, vol. 4, pp. 205-207). (It should be pointed out however that subjective interpretation includes, not just philosophical and theological exegeses, but also those with mystical tendencies.

Based on the definition offered for rational-theological exegesis, many exegeses fit this denomination. Of some of these exegeses, only their names remain, and of others there are only fragments extant, including a number strewn throughout other books. But there are a few that have been preserved intact, a number of which have undergone reprint.

The following is a list of the most influential theological exegeses arranged in chronological order.

The exegesis by Abū Bakr 'Abd al-Raḥmān ibn Kīsān al-Aṣamm (d. 200 or 201/815 or 816), the Mu'tazilī scholar and exeget whom Mu'tazilīs excommunicated for his Shī'a tendencies (Ibn Nadīm, Pers. tr., p. 214). Qāḍī 'Abd al-Jabbār Hamadānī assesses this exegesis as eccentric (*Faḍl al-I'tizāl*, p. 267).

Tafsīr al-Qur'an and *Ta'wīl al-Qur'an* both by the Mu'tazilī Ḍirār ibn 'Amr. He is a contemporary of Aḥmad ibn Ḥanbal, although evidently they suffered a strained relationship (Ibn Nadīm, Pers. tr., p. 215; Ibn Ḥajar 'Asqalānī, vol. 3, p. 203).

The exegesis by Abū 'Alī Jubbā'ī, a Mu'tazilī theologian (d. 303/915-916). Shaykh Ṭūsī, in the introduction to his exegesis *al-Tibyān* (vol. 1, p. 1), considers this work a theological exegesis, quoting from it frequently (e.g. vol. 1, p. 102, vol. 2, p. 12, vol. 5, p. 6). Ibn Ṭāwūs also quotes parts of this work (pp. 252-303). Daniel Zhīmārah reconstructed this exegesis in 1994. Also, Abū 'Alī Fārsī (d. 377/987-988), Persian philosologist and grammarian of Arabic, wrote an exposition of this exegesis entitled *al-Tatabbu' li-Kalām Abī 'Alī al-Jubbā'ī fī al-Tafsīr*, which was approximately one hundred pages in length (Yāqūt Ḥimawī, vol. 2, p. 814; Ṣafadī, vol. 11, p. 379; also see Ṣādiqī, pp. 551-557). Abū Hāshim Jubbā'ī (d. 321/933), the latter's son, also purportedly authored an exegesis on the Qur'an. Apparently, Suyūṭī (1960, p. 33) had seen some parts of this work, but there is no mention of it in any other source.

Al-Tafsīr al-Kabīr li- al-Qur'an by Abū al-Qāsim 'Abd Allāh ibn Aḥmad Ka'bī Balkhī (d. 319/931), the Mu'tazilī theologian, is also a theological exegesis (Ibn Nadīm, Pers. tr., p. 219). Ibn Ṭāwūs claims (p. 314) that the original name of this work was *Jāmi' 'Ilm al-Qur'an*, and Ṣafadī (vol. 17, p. 26) believes that it spanned twelve volumes. Ibn Ṭāwūs (pp. 315-337) and Shaykh Ṭūsī (vol. 5, pp. 27-29) relate excerpts from this work, criticising his views. In these excerpts, the rationalist tendency of the author, like other Mu'tazilīs, is evident.

Another theological exegesis is by Abū Muslim Muḥammad ibn Baḥr Iṣfahānī (d. 322/933-934) entitled *Jāmi' al-Ta'wīl li-Muḥkam al-Tanzīl*, which the author has written based on Mu'tazilī doctrine (Ibn Nadīm, Pers. tr., p. 151). According to Yaqūt Ḥamawī (vol. 6, p. 2438), it spanned fourteen volumes. Shaykh Ṭūsī (vol. 1, pp. 1-2), though praising it in general, finds it needlessly protracted. (for further details about the author's life and views, see Sarmadī, pp. 23-36.) Sa'īd al-Anṣārī, an Indian scholar, has collected the excerpts quoted from this exegesis in other books and has published them under the title *Multaqaṭ Jāmi' al-Ta'wīl li-Muḥkam al-Tanzīl* (Culcutta: 1921).

Abū al-Ḥasan 'Alī ibn Ismā'īl Ash'arī (d. 324/935-936), the founder of the Ash'arī school and a student of Abū 'Alī Jubbā'ī, also authored a voluminous exegesis on the Qur'an entitled *Kitāb fī Tafsīr al-Qur'an wa al-Radd 'alā Man Khālafa al-Bayān min Ahl al-Ifk wa al-Buhtān*, which later became known as *al-Mukhtazan* (Ibn Farḥūn, vol. 2, p. 95). In this work, 'Alī ibn Ismā'īl repudiates the Mu'tazilī exegeses written by such figures as Jubbā'ī and Abū al-Qāsim Balkhī. Ibn 'Asākir (pp. 136-139) relates the author's introduction in this exegesis.

Abū Manṣūr Muḥammad ibn Muḥammad Māturīdī Samarqandī (d. 333/944-945)—theologian, exeget, and the founder of the Māturīdiyya theological school—is the author of a Qur'anic exegesis, *Ta'wīlāt Ahl al-Sunna*, in which he interprets the Qur'an in conformity with his peculiar theological views. He also used this work to disprove the views of his adversaries. For instance, in relation to verse 8, sura al-Baqara (2) he disputes the Karrāmiyya's view regarding faith (*īmān*; vol. 1, p. 44), and on verse 24 of the same sura, he argues against the Mu'tazilī belief on the eternal chastisement in hellfire of the perpetrators of major sins (vol. 1, p. 73, 179).

Another theological exegesis is that by 'Alī ibn 'Īsā Rummānī (d. 384/994-995), the Mu'tazilī grammarian and exeget. In the introduction to his exegesis, Shaykh Ṭūsī (vol. 1, pp. 1-2), frowns on its prolixity, despite commending it in general. Ibn Ṭāwūs (pp. 394-397) records passages from this exegesis, occasionally critiquing Rummānī's views. Several manuscripts of this exegesis are preserved in libraries of different countries (Encyclopedia of Islam 2nd Edition, s.v. al-Rummānī).

Qāḍī 'Abd al-Jabbār Hamadānī (d. 415/1024-1025), the Mu'tazilī theologian and exeget, authored an independent work on Qur'anic exegesis entitled *Tanzīh al-Qur'an 'an al-Maṭā'in*, besides expressing his exegetic views in various works, including *al-Mughnī*. In this exegesis, he offers rational-theological expositions in response to questions posed to him regarding the meaning of certain verses. At the same time, he answers objections that may be raised by those opposed to the Mu'tazilīs, which in some cases requires resorting to subjective interpretation (*ta'wīl*; see above; Zurqānī, vol. 2, p. 74, Muḥammad Ḥusayn Dhahabī, vol. 1, pp. 390-401). For instance, in his exposition of 2:26 (p. 19), he postulates an explanation for the Mu'tazilī view on error (*ḍalāla*). Or, in the exegesis of 28:30 (p. 310), he defends the position on the temporal contingence (*ḥudūth*) of God's Word.

Another work that may be classified as a rational-theological exegesis is *Amālī* or, more accurately, *Ghurar al-Fawā'id wa Durar al-Qalā'id* by Sharīf Murtaḍā 'Allama al-Hudā (d. 436/1044-1045), Shī'a theologian and jurisprudent. This work contains eighty scholarly discussions on Qur'anic exegesis, hadith, and literature, and on numerous occasions the author offers theological comments on Qur'anic verses (e.g. part 1, pp. 25-48, 526-529).

Abū Yūsuf 'Abd al-Salām ibn Muḥammad ibn Yūsuf ibn Bundār Qazwīnī (d. 483/1090-1091), a student of Qāḍī 'Abd al-Jabbār, is the author of an extensive exegesis on the Qur'an entitled *Ḥadā'iq Dhāt Bahja fī Tafsīr al-Qur'an al-Karīm*. Regarding the length of this work, there is disagreement, with some estimating it between three hundred to seven hundred sections. His exegesis on sura al-Fātiḥa (1) extended over seven volumes, and his exegesis on 2:102 runs into an entire volume. In this exegesis, he employs the method of his Mu'tazilī predecessors (Rāfi'ī Qazwīnī, vol. 3, p. 178; Muḥammad ibn

Aḥmad Dhahabī, vol. 18, pp. 616-620; Ḥājī Khalīfa, vol. 1, col. 634). Sulaymān ibn Ḥasan Ṣahrishtī, Shī'a jurisprudent and theologian and a contemporary of Qazwīnī, criticises some of the latter's views in his *al-Naḍīr fī Naqḍ Kalām Ṣāḥib al-Tafsīr* (Ibn Shahr Āshūb, p. 56).

Abū Sa'd Muḥsin ibn Muḥammad, more commonly referred to as Ḥākim Jushamī, Zaydī scholar and theologian, is the author of a Qur'anic exegesis entitled *al-Tahdhīb fī Tafsīr al-Qur'an*. The theological significance of this work lies in its quotations of Mu'tazilī views (Zarzūr, pp. 161-162; Encyclopedia of Islam, 2nd edition, Supplements 5-6, s.v. al-Ḥākim al-Jushamī).

There are more exegeses preserved from the fifth/eleventh century onwards and these can be assessed with more confidence with the views of exegets of the period and their methodology. An important work of the fifth/eleventh century is *al-Tibyān fī Tafsīr al-Qur'an* by Shaykh Ṭūsī (d. 460/1067-1068), Shī'a jurisprudent, exeget, and theologian. This work is also significant in that it is the first complete Qur'anic exegesis by a Shī'a, and although it is replete with comments treating of literature, jurisprudence, and principles of jurisprudence, we may consider it a theological exegesis for its overall theological leaning (Ṭabāṭabā'ī, pp. 50-51). Ṭūsī in *al-Tibyān* often broaches theological topics in interpreting the verses of the Qur'an, on many occasions defending Shī'a tenets. In his exposition of 5:55, for instance, he argues in defense of 'Alī's status as the immediate successor of the Prophet. Or on 3:28, he argues for the Shī'a practice of discretionary concealment of beliefs (*taqīya*) when one's life is in danger (*al-Tibyān fī Tafsīr al-Qur'an*). Among the other theological features of this exegesis is his mention of the views of the Mu'tazilī and Ash'arī schools and his well-reasoned and rational arguments in replying to them (ibid.).

Another important theological exegesis is *Tafsīr al-Kashshāf 'an Ḥaqā'iq Ghawāmiḍ al-Tanzīl wa 'Uyūn al-Aqāwīl fī Wujūh al-Ta'wīl* by Jār Allāh Maḥmūd ibn 'Umar Zamakhsharī (d. 528/1133-1134), Mu'tazilī literary figure, exeget, and theologian.

Concerning this exegesis, Ibn Khaldūn states, "The author explicates the Muʿtazilī doctrine in his interpretation of Qur'anic verses. It is for this reason that scholars of the Sunnī [Ashʿarī] school have avoided it. But, if one is fully aware of the Sunnī doctrine and the ways of argumentation, then one would be immune to its Muʿtazilī views" (vol. 1, pp. 555-556). Kashshāf is often assailed with such language and criticism (e.g. Ibn Taymiyya, pp. 34, 51; Muḥammad Ḥusayn Dhahabī, vol. 1, pp. 435-442; see also al-Kashshāf ʿan Ḥaqā'iq al-Tanzīl). Nonetheless, even detractors appreciate its usefulness (Ibn Khaldūn, vol. 1, pp. 555-556, Muḥammad Ḥusayn Dhahabī, vol. 1, pp. 435-442). Among the features of this exegesis is the presentation of Muʿtazilī views, which the author elucidates in numerous examples. For instance, in the exposition of 1:10, wherein there is mention of "God's Hand," Zamakhsharī argues against anthropomorphism; in commenting on 14:22, he rejects predestination; and in his exposition of 2:3, 3:173, and 53:33, he postulates the Muʿtazilī doctrine of the station between two stations (manzilah bayna manzilatayn; for further details on Zamakhsharī's Muʿtazilī views as reflected in his exegesis, see Ḥawfī, pp. 122-166; Fāḍil, pp. 318-336). Numerous exegeses have been written on al-Kashshāf, primarily among them being al-Inṣāf fī Mā Taḍammanahu al-Kashshāf min al-Iʿtizāl by Egyptian Mālikī exeget and jurisprudent, Abū al-ʿAbbās Aḥmad ibn Manṣūr Judhāmī Jaramī, otherwise known as Ibn Munayyir (d. 683/1284-1285). This has been repeatedly published along with al-Kashshāf as marginalia (for further details onother commentaries and super-commentaries on al-Kashshāf, see Ḥājī Khalīfa, vol. 2, cols. 1477-1484, and for Shīʿa commentaries and supre-comentaries, see Āqā Buzurg Ṭihrānī, vol. 3, pp. 30, 332, 420, vol. 4, pp. 310, 425, vol. 5, p. 99, vol. 6, pp. 46, 59).

A very prominent theological exegesis of the Qur'an is Mafātīḥ al-Ghayb or, as it is more popularly referred to, Tafsīr Kabīr by the Ashʿarī theologian and Qur'anic exeget, Fakhr al-Dīn Muḥammad ibn ʿUmar Rāzī (d. 604/1207-1208). By virtue of its extensive coverage of theological questions, some have termed it an encyclopedia of theology (Muḥammad Ḥusayn Dhahabī, vol. 1, p. 295; Shaḥḥāta, p. 163). Fakhr al-Dīn engages in interpreting the Qur'an with a rationalist approach and in his treatment alludes to numerous other disciplines and sciences of his day (Shaḥāta, p. 163). As such, his exegesis abounds with quotations from philosophers and sages as well as intellectual disputation (Biltājī, p. 120). Fakhr Rāzī presents his discussions on a particular verse in an orderly fashion, and when attempting to refute the views of his adversaries from among the Muʿtazilīs and the Karrāmiyya, he elucidates them at length (Muḥammad Ḥusayn Dhahabī, vol. 1, pp. 294-295; Biltājī, p. 126). As previously raised, one of the features of this exegesis is Fakhr Rāzī's mention of the rationalist views and arguments of the philosophers. In his exposition of 2:48, for instance, he explains the interpretation of philosophers on the doctrine of intercession (*Tafsīr Kabīr*).

In more recent times, many rational-theological exegeses have been produced. These include the following titles: *Tafsīr Rūḥ al-Maʿānī* by Shihāb al-Dīn Maḥmūd Ālūsī Baghdādī (d. 1270/1853-1854); *Tafsīr al-Qur'an al-Ḥakīm* (more often referred to as *Tafsīr al-Khafājī*) by Muḥammad ʿAbd al-Munʿim Khafājī (d. 1328 /1910-1911); *Taḥrīr al-Maʿānī al-Sadīd wa Tanwīr al-ʿAql al-Jadīd* (more popularly known by its abridged title, *al-Taḥrīr wa al-Tanwīr*) by Muḥammad Ṭāhir ibn ʿĀshūr (d. 1352 AHS/1933-1934), Tunisian scholar from the Mālikī school; *al-Mīzān fī Tafsīr al-Qur'an* by Muḥammad Ḥusayn Ṭabāṭabā'ī (d. 1361 AHS/1982), the Shīʿa exeget and philosopher, who in the course of his exegesis argues in defense of Shīʿa tenets while also dwelling on philosophical and social topics; *Ālā' al-Raḥmān fī Tafsīr al-Qur'an* by Shaykh Muḥammad Jawād Balāghī (d. 1352/1933-1934), Shīʿa exeget, theologian, and literary figure; *Aṭyab al-Bayān fī Tafsīr al-Qur'an* by the Shīʿa theologian, Sayyid ʿAbd al-Ḥusayn Ṭayyib Iṣfahānī (1369 AHS/1949-1950).

Theological exegeses also appear in another form comprising

those authored by members of various schools and sects in which they offer their theological views. The Ibāḍīs (an offshoot of the Khārijī sect) have, for instance, produced a number of Qur'anic exegeses; the most prominent being *Tafsīr Kitāb Allāh al-'Azīz* (Beirut: 1990) by Hūd ibn Muḥakkam Huwārī, exeget of the third century affiliated with the Ibāḍī school. This exegesis is composed in the main of transmitted material, and may thus be classified as transmitted interpretation. However, the author propounds in the course of his work his theological views on such issues as faith and unfaith, perpetration of major sins, and intercession (Ayāzī, 1374 AHS/1995), pp. 147-148). In this regard, one may also point to *Hamyān al-Zād ilā Dār al-Ma'ād* (Amman: 1401-1411/1991) and *Taysīr al-Tafsīr* (Amman: 1407-1409/1987-1989) both by Muḥammad ibn Yūsuf Aṭfīsh (d. 1332/1913-1914).

As regards exegeses by the Zaydiyya, one may name *Tafsīr Fatḥ al-Qadīr al-Jāmi' bayn Fannay al-Riwāya wa al-Dirāya min 'Ilm al-Tafsīr* (Beirut, n.d.) by Muḥammad ibn 'Alī ibn 'Abd Allāh Shawkānī (d. 1250/1834-1835). This is in addition to *Tafsīr Gharīb al-Qur'an* (Qum: 1414/1991) purportedly by Zayd ibn 'Alī and the exegesis by Muqātil ibn Sulaymān (Cairo: 1979-1989), both of which are credited to the Zaydī school (Shaḥāta, p. 190).

The Ismā'īlīs have not produced a complete and exhaustive Qur'anic exegesis, although Qāḍī Nu'mān (d. 363/973-974) in his works—such as *al-Majālis wa al-Musāyarāt* (Tunisia: 1978)—and Mu'ayyad fī al-Dīn Hiba Allāh Shīrāzī in his *al-Majlis al-Mu'ayyada* (Beirut: 1974) dwell on various verses related to the topics of their books (for more examples, see Muḥammad Ḥusayn Dhahabī, vol. 2, pp. 258-274; Poonawala, pp. 199-222). Furthermore, assuming concurrence with those claiming Muḥammad ibn 'Abd al-Karīm Shahristānī (d. 548/1153-1154)—author of the esteemed *al-Milal wa al-Niḥal*—was Ismā'īlī (Ibn Ḥajar 'Asqalānī, vol. 5, p. 263; Bahrāmī, pp. 356-381), his exegesis entitled *Mafātīḥ al-Asrār wa Maṣābīḥ al-Abrār* (Tehran: 1376 AHS/1997) may be added to the list of Ismā'īlī exegeses on the Qur'an.

Certain Muslim philosophers have also employed the rationalist approach and philosophical themes in composing Qur'anic exegeses, such as Avicenna in his exposition of Suras Tawḥīd, Falaq, Nās, and A'lā (1, 113, 114, 87; for further details onthis topic, see *Ḥikmat*, pp. 159-174). Shihāb al-Dīn Suhrawardī (d. 587/1191-1192) also indulges in exegesis of numerous verses throughout his works and especially in his *al-Talwīḥāt al-Lawḥiyya wa al-'Arshiyya* (*Majmū'i-yi Muṣannafāt*, vol. 1, pp. 83, 92-93). Muḥammad ibn Ibrāhīm Shīrāzī, otherwise known as Mullā Ṣadrā (d. 1050/1640-1641), has also produced Qur'anic exegesis. His *Tafsīr al-Qur'an al-Karīm* (Qum: 1379 AHS/2000) and *Mafātīḥ al-Ghayb* (Tehran: 1363 AHS/1983) are both works in which the author approaches Qur'anic verses in view of his distinctive philosophical outlook (Mullā Ṣadrā›s Exegesis).

10. MYSTICAL EXEGESIS OF THE QUR'AN

Muḥsin Qāsimpūr

Mystical exegesis rests on extracting esoteric meaning from Qur'anic verses regardless of their apparent meaning. This perception is rooted in a certain view that conceives one or multiple layers of esoteric meaning transcending the literal meaning, revealed exclusively by way of mystical unveiling. This conception of the Qur'an differs from the standard approach to Qur'anic exegesis and is based on distinct principles (Suyūṭī, 1363 AHS/1983), vol. 4, pp. 200-205; 'Akk, p. 30).According to one definition, mystical exegesis comprises the inward intuitions of the mystic (Zarkashī, vol. 2, p. 311; Suyūṭī, 1363 AHS/1983, vol. 4, p. 224) and as such is the product of the mystic's reflections and inferences deriving from his mystical perception and experience. Based on other definitions, mystical exegesis is a metaphorical, figurative, and occult construal of the Qur'an but is disapproved by jurisprudents, who understand Qur'anic verses largely in the context of their literal, scientific, and jurisprudential signification (Blachère, p. 219).

Mystical exegesis is alternatively referred to as allegorical and symbolic interpretation. As such, it does depend on the Qur'anic text (Encyclopedia of Religion, vol. 14, p. 239). By virtue of its approach, mystical exegesis bears more affinity to certain philosophical and theological schools such as the Shī'a school (Metz, Pers. tr., vol. 1, p. 227; see also Ta'wīl).

Scholars disagree as to the validity of such exegesis. Some condemn it as invalid and even heretical (Ibn Ṣalāḥ, vol. 1, pp. 196-197, Zarkashī, vol. 2, p. 311). These condemnations are opposed and justification is given to such exegeses (Taftāzānī, pp. 189-190; Zurqānī, vol. 2, pp. 89-90; Aṭīṣ, Pers. tr., pp. 14-15) with a prerequisite that exegetic principles are fully complied with and association is provided to mystical exegesis by way of juxtaposing the literal meaning of verses and their esoteric allusions. This recognition can only be granted, according to Suyūṭī (1363 AHS/1983), when it is further strengthened through the perfection of faith and gnosis (Suyūṭī, vol. 4, p. 224). 'Abd al-Wahhāb Sha'rānī (vol. 1, p. 4) states that such exegesis is valid, for mystics may attain to meaning that is beyond the ken of those who confine themselves to the exoteric aspect of religion.

The history of mystical exegesis may be traced to the formative period of Islam, during the Prophet's lifetime (Hujwīrī, p. 50; Aṭīṣ, Pers. tr., pp. 20-26). The verses cited by Sufis to substantiate their view (e.g., Qur'an 4:80, 47:24, 2:115,156, 24:35) came also to serve as a basis for mystical exegesis (Abū Naṣr Sarrāj, pp. 105-106; Shāṭibī, vol. 3, pp. 382-383; Goldziher, Arab. tr., pp 204-205). What helped in entrenching this reasoning was the presence of figurative expressions in the Qur'an, which, according to Suyūṭī (1363 AHS/1983, vol. 3, p. 120) is indubitable, and without which the Qur'an would lack a substantial source of its beauty (e.g. 2:74, 187, 6:132, 7:175-176, 25:12, 19:4, 36:37, 48:29, 61:46).

There are reports attributed to some prominent Companions expressing that the literal meaning of Qur'anic verses is not the only meaning intended (Ibn Ḥanbal, vol. 1, p. 79; Abū Ṭālib

Makkī, vol. 1, p. 49). Prior to the composition of mystical exegeses, there was a well-known and oft-cited saying by Ibn 'Abbās concerning verse the Qur'an, 66:12—"Should I express its interpretation, you would stone me to death, i.e., you would condemn me as a disbeliever"—(Muḥammad Ghazālī, 1412/1992, vol. 4, p. 356). There were also individuals during the period of the Successors, such as Ḥasan Baṣrī, who interpreted the Qur'an with an allegorical (*ishārī*) approach (*Atış*, Pers. tr., p. 31).

Paul Noya is of the opinion (Pers. tr., pp. 136-139, 146) that the first instances of mystical exegesis are perceivable in the teachings of Imām Ṣādiq, concerning the occult science of *jafr* and mystical experience as recorded in Sulamī's *Ḥaqā'iq al-Tafsīr*, though the ascription of these sayings is dubious (Subḥānī, p. 99). Paul Noya further writes (Pers. tr., p. 98) that the mythological and metaphorical vein in which Muqātil ibn Sulaymān (d. 150/767-768) wrote his *al-Tafsīr al-Kabīr* became a source of inspiration for such mystics as Ḥakīm Tirmidhī (d. 285/898-899; cf. Subḥānī, pp. 97-99).

In the mystical exegesis, the mystic offers interpretations that diverge from the literal meaning of the verses of the Qur'an, based on mystical principles or spiritual intuition that come from his esoteric experience. The distinctive feature of this genre of exegesis is its employment of the allegorical language and the peculiar parlance necessitated by the nature of spiritual experience (Mustamlī, vol. 3, pp. 1160-1161; Aḥmad Ghazālī, annotated by Pūrjavādī, pp. 73-74). For this reason, mystical exegesis is referred to by some as allegorical exegesis (Qushayrī, vol. 1, p. 41; Suyūṭī, 1363 AHS/1983, vol. 4, p. 224; Zurqānī, vol. 2, p. 78; *Atış*, Pers. tr., p. 12). These allegorical insights are in some cases reconcilable with the literal meaning of verses (Zurqānī, vol. 2, p. 78). Ibn 'Arabī states that the method pursued by mystics in explicating the meaning of Revelation is an allegory, and the reason why the people of truth (*ahl al-ḥaqīqa*) designate the meaning they arrive at as such is out of fear of being persecuted by jurists and scholars whose understanding is limited to the exoteric (*al-Futūḥāt al-Makkiyya*, vol. 1, p. 279).

Sayyid Ḥaydar Āmulī maintains (1416/1996, vol. 1, p. 206) that the esoteric meaning of the Divine verses (*āyāt*) disclosed by mystics is in essence the introspective interpretation (*tafsīr anfusī*), i.e.,, it is an illustration of the existing harmony between the macrocosm (*āfāq*) and the microcosm, the mystic's inner self (*anfus*), an understanding derived from this verse: *Soon We shall show them Our signs in the horizons and in their own souls until it becomes clear to them that He is the Real. Is it not sufficient that your Lord is witness to all things?* (Qur'an 41:53) As such, this perspective draws a parallel between the book of creation (the macrocosm) and the book of revelation (the Qur'an), and this is made possible by the introspective interpretation or *ta'wīl*.

This distinct approach is underpinned by distinctive ontological and epistemological principles postulated by the mystics. Mystics assert that the world of existence has an outward and an inward reality and that there is a perpetual process in which the inward surfaces become the outward and the outward retreats again into the inward. Like respiration, existence inhales and exhales (Ibn 'Arabī, *al-Futūḥāt Makkiyya*, vol. 2, pp. 391-392; Shabistarī, pp. 67-68). The human being, like the cosmos, is composed of a body and a soul, the body being the outward existence and the soul the inward existence (Najm Rāzī, p. 311; Rumi, vol. 2, Book Three, line 4248). This view concerning the similarity between the human being and the Qur'an in subsuming an inward and an outward aspect is also espoused by certain philosophers (Ṣadr al-Dīn Shīrāzī, p. 23; Shāygān, p. 110).

A number of hadiths corroborate this construal by stating that the Qur'an has an inward aspect as well as an outward aspect and that it contains definition (*ḥadd*) and prelude (*maṭla'*). Based on these hadiths, every verse possesses both an inward and an outward aspect, and every letter in the Qur'an has a definition and every every definition has a prelude (Ṣaffār Qummī, p. 223; 'Ayyāshī, vol. 1, pp. 86-87; Suyūṭī, 1363 AHS/1983, vol. 4, p. 225; Majlisī, vol. 89, p. 94).

A hadith from Imām Ṣādiq explains that the Qur'an subsumes four strata: expressions (*'ibārāt*), allusions (*ishārāt*), subtleties (*laṭā'if*), and truths (*ḥaqā'iq*; Āmulī, 1368 AHS/1989), p. 530; Majlisī, vol. 89, p. 103). Citing such hadiths, mystics hold that beyond the literal meaning of the words, there exists a deeper meaning, a 'sensus plenior,' incorporating up to seven strata of meaning (Āmulī, 1353 AHS/1975), vol. 1, p. 12; idem, 1368 AHS/1989, p. 530). Mystics invoke such hadiths to validate and corroborate their exegetic principles.

Abū Naṣr Sarrāj (pp. 105-106) devotes in his book a section entitled Inferences (*mustanbaṭāt*) on the topic of the inward and outward meanings of the Qur'an. He comes to the conclusion that the Qur'an as well as the Prophetic actions and sayings (*sunna*) possess an outward and an inward meaning. Abū Ṭālib Makkī (vol. 1, pp. 156-157) offers evidence in support of this position but goes further to affirm the superiority of the esoteric knowledge over the exoteric. Ibn 'Arabī (*al-Futūḥāt Makkiyya*, vol. 1, p. 279) is also of the conviction that every verse in the Qur'an contains two existential aspects; one is the inward, which can be perceived only by the "people of the truth" reflected in the mirror of their hearts, and the other comprises the words and phrases, which exists in the apparent outside the hearts of the "people of the truth."

Mystical exegesis is of two types: inspirational allegorical and that based on theoretical mysticism (Dhahabī, vol. 2, p. 368). Some Qur'anic scholars, however, object to this bifurcation, asserting that the only difference among mystical interpretations is in their "intensity and weakness" (Ma'rifat, vol. 2, pp. 538-539).

The Prophetic traditions (*sunna*) interpretation is a method whereby mystics interpret the Qur'an in deviation from its literal meaning and in accordance with the hidden and secret allegories. This method does not presuppose any of the concepts of theoretical mysticism and may in most cases be justified by the literal meaning. It is in essence an attempt at a merger between the exoteric aspect of religion (*sharī'a*) and the esoteric aspect of religion (*ḥaqīqa*; Suyūṭī, 1960, p. 21). Though this form of interpretation is symbolic, it is considered a valid form of interpretation since the interpreters strive to construe verses in their context and in accord with the Prophetic traditions (Zarrīnkūb, vol. 1, p. 348). The main element in the inspirational-allegorical interpretation is spiritual exercise, enabling the mystic to achieve spiritual unveiling and a deep self awareness. These mystic exegetes postulate a multiplicity of meanings existing beyond the literal meaning (Dhahabī, vol. 2, pp. 381-382). The inspirational-allegorical interpretation should not be conflated with esoteric exegeses, which are a form of exegeses that posit baseless claims (*Atış*, Pers. tr., pp. 16-17), although inspirational-allegorical exegesis does invoke the principles of practical Sufism for interpreting the Qur'an (Qushayrī, vol. 2, pp. 131, 316-317, 407; Miybudī, vol. 10, p. 654).

Some Sufis underscore that the literal meaning should not be neglected under the pretext of interpretation. As such, they make a point of differentiating between this form of interpretation and the esoteric forms proffered by certain philosophers, theologians, and esotericists (*bāṭiniyya*; Muḥammad Ghazālī, 1412/1992, vol. 1, p. 49; idem1407/1987, p. 160; see also Miybudī, vol. 5, p. 307; Surūsh, pp. 396-399). According to these Sufis, the univocal and the prescriptive verses are excluded (Zarrīnkūb, vol. 2, p. 349) and that mystical interpretations are restricted to the equivocal verses and those verses pertaining to human being and cosmic mysteries.

The exegesis by Sahl Tustarī (d. 283/896-897) is recognised as among the earliest prototypes of inspirational-allegorical interpretation and has great influence on later Sufi exegets. Abū 'Abd al-Raḥmān Sulamī, for instance, draws on Tustarī's work in his *Ḥaqā'iq al-Tafsīr* (Bowering, p. 112).

Sulamī's *Ḥaqā'iq al-Tafsīr* is also an important work in the inspirational-allegorical vein that influenced such later exegeses as *Laṭā'if al-Ishārāt* by Qushayrī (d. 465/1072-1073; Qushayrī, vol. 1, Basyūnī's introduction, p. 11). Sulamī's exegesis is a compilation of interpretations ascribed to Imām Ṣādiq, Abū al-Ḥusayn Nūrī (d. 295/907-908), Ḥusayn ibn Manṣūr Ḥallāj (d. 309/921-922), and Ibn 'Aṭā (d. 309/921-922; Sulamī, vol. 1, Pūrjavādī's introduction, pp. XIV-XV). Qushayrī's *Laṭā'if al-Ishārāt* is also an inspirational-allegorical exegesis (Ibn 'Arabī, *Qānūn al-Ta'wīl*, p. 207).

Muḥammad Ḥusayn Dhahabī (vol. 2, pp. 412-443) and Muḥammad Hādī Ma'rifat (vol. 2, pp. 539-588) have listed important Qur'anic exegeses written in the inspirational-allegorical vein. Rashīd Aḥmad (p. 57) considers *Laṭā'if al-Ishārāt* by Qushayrī, a Sufi and a theologian, as the first proper mystical exegesis, stating that the works by Sulamī and Tustarī fail to meet the criteria of mystical exegesis. Later exegets viewed Qushayrī's exegesis as a credible source. Rūzbahān Baqlī Shīrāzī (d. 606/1209-1210), for instance, counts Qushayrī's exegesis as one of his sources in writing *'Arā'is al-Bayān fī Ḥaqā'iq al-Qur'an*. Muḥammad ibn Yūsuf Ḥusaynī (d. 825/1421-1422), also known as Gīsūdirāz, an Indian Sufi and mystic, quotes from Qushayrī in his *al-Multaqaṭ*, albeit without specifying his name (Rashīd Aḥmad, pp. 67-68).

The unpublished *al-Fuṣūl* by Abū Ḥanīfa 'Abd al-Wahhāb ibn Muḥammad is a work that accommodates both mystic and theological tendencies in the Karrāmiyya School. This work is distinguished by its treatment of the views of Muḥammad ibn Karrām and other Karrāmī scholars and mystics, and it succeeds in offering a relatively realistic picture of Karrāmiyya doctrine (Shafī'ī Kadkanī, pp. 61-113).

Kashf al-Asrār wa 'Udda al-Abrār (composed in 520/1126-1127) by Rashīd al-Dīn Miybudī is another mystical exegesis written in Persian. In elucidating his method, the author writes (vol. 1, p. 1) that he first offers a translation of a verse, then its interpretation, and finally its esoteric meaning. The author devotes the third phase of his exegesis to the mystic tradition and the ways of the Sufis.

One may also point to *'Arā'is al-Bayān fī Ḥaqā'iq al-Qur'an* by

Rūzbahān Baqlī as another mystical exegesis. The author, while mentioning in passing the exoteric meaning of verses, pursues in most cases an intuitive allegorical approach with an esoteric inclination (Junayd Shīrāzī, p. 244; Munzavī, vol. 1, p. 170; *Rūzbahān-nāma*, Dānishpazhūh's introduction, p. 8; Ṣāwī, p. 12).

Baḥr al-Ḥaqā'iq wa al-Ma'ānī fī Tafsīr al-Sab' al-Mathānī by Najm al-Dīn Rāzī, otherwise known as Najm al-Dīn Dāya, is a mystical exegesis encompassing up to 51:18. This exegesis pursues simultaneously the esoteric and exoteric meanings while striving to corroborate the principles of Sufism. Najm al-Dīn Dāya's work was subsequently taken up by 'Alā' al-Dawla Simnānī (Dhahabī, vol. 2, pp. 429-430; *Atış*, Pers. tr., p. 145).

Rumi's *Mathnawī Ma'nawī* may also be classified as mystical exegesis of the Qur'an for its treatment of the esoteric and exoteric interpretation of a large number of Qur'anic verses (Zarrīnkūb, vol. 2, p. 373).

Ismā'īl ibn Muṣṭafā Ḥaqqī wrote his exegesis, *Rūḥ al-Bayān*, in the intuitive (*dhawqī*) vein by drawing on such prior mystical exegeses as *Ta'wīlāt* by 'Abd al-Razzāq Kāshānī and *Baḥr al-Ḥaqā'iq wa al-Ma'ānī fī Tafsīr al-Sab' al-Mathānī* and benefitting from the mystical poetry of Rumi, Ḥāfiẓ, and Sa'dī (vol. 3, pp. 450, 453, vol. 6, pp. 177, 188, 201).

Bayān al-Sa'āda by Ḥājj Mullā Sulṭān Muḥammad Gunābādī, more commonly known as Sulṭān 'Alīshāh, (d. 1327/1909-1910) is also in the inspirational-allegorical denomination (for more examples of this exegetic approach, see Rūmī, vol. 1, p. 376).

With regard to inspirational-allegorical exegeses, one may point to those that consider only one sura or even one verse. Worthy of note here are *Mishkāh al-Anwār wa Muṣaffāh al-Asrār* by Imām Muḥammad Ghazālī (d. 505/1111) on 24:35, *Baḥr al-Maḥabba fī Asrār al-Mawadda* by Aḥmad Ghazālī (d. 520/1126-1127), *al-Sittīn al-Jāmi' li-Laṭā'if al-Basātīn* by Aḥmad ibn Muḥammad ibn Zayd Ṭūsī (fl. six/twelfth century), and *Ḥadā'iq al-Ḥaqā'iq* by Mu'īn al-Dīn Farāhī Hirawī, more commonly known as Mullā Miskīn (a mystic of the tenth/

sixteenth century; the latter three are in Persian and pertain to sura Yūsuf; *Atış*, Pers. tr., pp. 56-257).

Qur'anic interpretation based on theoretical mysticism developed under the influence of the works of Ibn 'Arabī and especially his principle of oneness of existence (*waḥdat wujūd*). Ṣadr al-Dīn Qūnawī (d. 673/1274-1275), Ibn 'Arabī's disciple and godson, and 'Abd al-Razzāq Kāshānī both followed Ibn 'Arabī in their Qur'anic exegeses. The main purpose in this approach is to verify the principles of theoretical mysticism by invoking Qur'anic verses (Ma'rifat, vol. 2, p. 577, *Atış*, Pers. tr., p. 174). The exegesis *Raḥma min al-Raḥmān*, a compilation of the exegetic views of Ibn Arabī constructed from his various works on the Qur'an and mysticism (e.g. *I'jāz al-Bayān fī al-Tarjama 'an al-Qur'an*, *al-Jam' wa al-Tafṣīl fī Asrār Ma'ānī al-Tanzīl*, and *al-Futūḥāt al-Makkiyya*) is one such work (Ma'rifat, vol. 2, p. 572). (Some have speculated that in postulating oneness of existence, Ibn 'Arabī was influenced by Ibn Barrajān, d. 536/1141-1142; *Atış*, Pers. tr., p. 125).

Other important and renowned examples of Qur'anic exegeses based on theoretical mysticism are *I'jāz al-Bayān fī Kashf Ba'd Asrār Umm al-Qur'an* by Ṣadr al-Dīn Qūnawī on sura al-Ḥamd (1) and *Tafsīr al-Qur'an al-Karīm* by 'Abd al-Razzāq Kāshānī, and a treatise on the esoteric significance of the verse *bi-'sm-i 'llāh* by Dāwūd Qayṣarī, who wrote a commentary on Ibn 'Arabī's *Fuṣūṣ al-Ḥikam*. Sayyid Ḥaydar Āmulī's *Tafsīr al-Muḥīṭ al-A'ẓam* is another prominent work premised on Ibn 'Arabī teachings. In this work, the author brings the Shī'a and the Sufi traditions together. This exegesis subsumes, according to its author, the esoteric (*ta'wīl*) and exoteric (*tafsīr*) or, in other words, the canon or the exoteric (*sharī'a*), the esoteric (*ṭarīqa*), and the ultimate reality, transcending even the esoteric (*ḥaqīqa*; vol. 1, p. 195).

11. SCIENTIFIC EXEGESIS OF THE QUR'AN

Shādī Nafīsī

In this approach, the exeget's purpose is to relate the verses of the Qur'an to the empirical findings of the sciences. Scholars have proffered different descriptions of this method, depending on whether they endorse it or not, but in most cases, reference is made to the discussion furnished by Imām Muḥammad Ghazālī (d. 505/1111) and the critique leveled by Abū al-Qāsim Shāṭibī (d. 590/1193-1194). Neither of these two pioneering scholars produced Qur'anic exegeses, Nevertheless in treating necessary disciplines required for a correct understanding of the Qur'an, they broached the question of whether exegets may be justified in having recourse to sciences that did not exist during the Period of Revelation. Ghazālī is in favor of employing such sciences, and following his lead, Zarkashī (d. 794/1391-1392) and Suyūṭī (d. 911/1505-1506) provide arguments in support of this position. They cite *al-Tafsīr al-Kabīr* by Fakhr Rāzī (d. 606/1209-1210) as a clear example of this method of Qur'anic exegesis. Shāṭibī was the first to challenge this position, and more recent exegets, such as Amīn Khūlī, have articulated their opposition to this method based on Shāṭibī's views, though in a somewhat more modern fashion (Rūmī, vol. 2, p. 572; Sharīf, p. 627; Sharqāwī, p. 393).

The earliest definition of scientific exegesis in recent times is that formulated by Amīn Khūlī, and other scholars have employed this definition with slight modifications (Dhahabī, vol. 2, p. 519; Muḥtasib, p. 247; Rūmī, vol. 2, p. 548). As the critics see it, in this method of Qur'anic exegesis, the Qur'an is of secondary rather than of primary concern, and for this reason, they deem it unacceptable (Abū Ḥujr, p. 66). The proponents of this method, however, invoke the scientific inimitability of the Qur'an and its applicability to all times and places (Rūmī, vol. 2, p. 549) or its allowance of deriving scientific propositions from it (Bakrī, p. 125). But these are disputed claims. A principal error in these definitions is that they wrongly conflate philosophy with science. Whereas science in its broadest meaning encompasses not only philosophy but the entire body of human knowledge, and as such may designate all types of Qur'anic with the only exception being intuitive exegesis (*tafsīr dhawqī*). In its more restricted denotation, science is seen entirely distinct from philosophy and excluding all philosophical conjecture (Rūmī, vol. 2, pp. 545-549).

The scientific approach to Qur'anic exegesis seems to have been inspired by the empirical milieu that prevailed in the modern West. This was the result of a generally positive susceptibility toward science and the future of humankind warranted by the impressive scientific developments of the age (Barbour, Pers. tr., p. 321). The world of Islam, in its confrontation with the progressive and dominant West, was strongly impressed by the milieu. So much so that being scientific was equated with being right; Islam's detractors would slate it as unscientific and its adherents would defend it as scientific. This approach is discernible in the words of the pioneering Muslim reformers of this era, such as Sayyid Jamāl al-Dīn Asadābādī (Mujtahidī, p.

23) and Sir Sayyid Aḥmad Khān (Akram, Pers. tr., p. 89; Nadawī, Pers. tr., p. 127). Ṭanṭāwī, whose Qur'anic exegesis, *al-Jawāhir*, stands out as the epitome of scientific exegesis, blaming the debasement and decadence of the Muslim world entirely on their weak foothold in science (vol. 1. pp. 35-36, vol. 17, p. 17, vol. 25, pp. 56-57). He describes his attempt at Qur'anic exegesis as a way of introducing science into the life of Muslims (vol. 2, p. 204). As such, it was the concern of certain Muslim intellectuals that gave rise to scientific exegesis, and so as this concern abated and as new topics surfaced (in Iran, for example, the focus shifted to such political topics as governance, freedom, and the scope of the government's power), interest in this genre of Qur'anic exegesis naturally declined.

In any case, the scientific approach to Qur'anic exegesis may be characterised as an effect of the reformation in religious thought in modern times. This approach is on full display in Ṭanṭāwī's *al-Jawāhir*, which is the only complete Qur'anic exegesis written in this genre. However, the influence of this approach is clearly evident in such works as *Tafsīr-i Nimūna* that take on a combination of approaches (Nafīsī, pp. 219-224; Ṭanṭāwī's Tafsīr). This approach has also produced numerous shorter works, which may be classified as thematic exegeses or otherwise seen as miscellaneous articles (e.g. Sharīf, pp. 723-724; Sharqāwī, pp. 423-424; Rūmī, vol. 2, pp. 604-615). Abundant examples of such works have been produced in Iran, which include, among others, works by such prominent figures as Mahdī Bāzargān, Pāknizhād, Makārim Shīrāzī, and Bīāzār Shīrāzī.

Due attention, however, must be mindfully paid to the few works of earlier origin that belong to this genre. Fakhr Rāzī in his *Tafsīr Kabīr* is primarily a theological exegesis but may also be designated as a scientific exegesis. It strives to show the consistency of the sciences of his time with the Qur'an (Fakhr Rāzī, vol. 2, pp. 102, 156). This observation should make it clear that invoking empirical science in commenting on the Qur'an does have precedence in earlier works. But as an independent genre, it is a more distinct feature of the modern times.

A central question concerning scientific exegesis is its validity and necessity. This approach has been evaluated both positively and negatively by various scholars and on differing grounds: Some have discussed it based on epistemological and linguistic premises; some have gauged it in accordance with the requisite criteria of proper exegesis; and some have considered the ramifications of this approach. In spite of this, all those who have examined this approach agree that God has two books: one is composed of words, which is the Qur'an, and the other comprises the natural phenomena. According to the Qur'an, both signify God (Waḥīd Akhtar, Pers. tr., pp. 55-56, 68; Sharīf, pp. 630-631; Rashīd Riḍā, vol. 2, p. 64; Ṭanṭāwī ibn Jawharī, vol. 2, p. 51). As such, care must be taken to avoid misunderstanding the debate over this approach as implying that religion and science are antithetical. What this debate concerns is strictly whether it is justifiable to employ empirical science in understanding the Qur'an.

Ghazālī, the earliest scholar whose words have been interpreted as favoring scientific exegesis of the Qur'an, raises this discussion when he considers the epistemological basis of the Qur'an. He maintains that the Qur'an contains all the knowledge that humankind may attain, including the empirical sciences. To corroborate his view, he cites some examples (Ghazālī (1412/1992), vol. 1, p. 383 idem, 1360 AHS/1981, p. 31). In his reasoning, Ghazālī (1412/1992, vol. 1, p. 383) lists a number of hadiths rather than Qur'anic verses. The most convincing of these is a discontinued (*mawqūf*) hadith from Ibn Mas'ūd: "He who seeks the knowledge of the people of the former times and of the people of later times should reflect on the Qur'an." Zarkashī, when speaking of the Qur'anic sciences, concurs with Ghazālī (Zarkashī, vol. 2, pp. 290-291). In support of his predecessors, Suyūṭī (vol. 4, pp. 28-29) cites the following two verses: 1. *We have not omitted anything from the Book* (6:38); 2. *We have sent down the Book to you as a clarification of all things* (16:89).

The doctrinal reasoning offered by modern advocates of

scientific exegesis are the same as those articulated by early proponents of this approach, deeming the Qur'an as containing all the sciences (Nawfal, p. 23; Ḥanafī Aḥmad, pp. 5-6). This approach has been criticised from a variety of aspects. The meaning of the cited verses from the Qur'an has been disputed, while the scope of the Qur'an's function has been confined by critics of this approach to the guidance of humankind (Shaltūt, p. 11). The hadiths adduced by the advocates of this approach have been discredited as apocryphal (Ghazālī, 1412/1991, vol. 1, p. 384, n. 1, 3). Furthermore, the proponents have not been able to provide sufficient proof to substantiate their claim to the comprehensiveness of the Qur'an. The construal assigned to a few verses that allegedly concern empirical science, in addition to being limited to merely a few scientific topics (Ghazālī, 1412/1991, vol. 1, p. 383; idem, 1360 AHS/1981, p. 31), are, at least in some cases, inconsistent and inappropriate (Suyūṭī, vol. 4, pp. 30-33, where he quotes from a person by the name of Abū al-Faḍl al-Mursī). Many of the instances that Ṭanṭāwī claims to be related to certain sciences are unacceptable (Nafīsī, pp. 151-155). This opinion is upheld in the theological argument enunciated by the proponents—to the effect that Islam is an all-encompassing religion and as such must express whatever leads to human gain or loss (Rūmī, vol. 2, p. 575, apud 'Abd al-'Azīz ibn Khalaf).

Some reasoning is that if the correct approach is taken when reading the Qur'an and treating of verses that speak of creation as seriously as those in dealing with religious injunctions, from which we derive new injunctions, we could arrive at new scientific findings (Ṭanṭāwī ibn Jawharī, vol. 3, p. 19, vol. 5, p. 56; Ḥanafī Aḥmad, p. 36; Jawādī Āmulī, p. 182). It can be ascertained from this opinion that dissimilarities do not exist between the discipline of jurisprudence—which is of a legal nature and formulates injunctions governing the individual and society—and empirical science, which seeks to understand the existential relation among natural phenomena. Another point overlooked is that even in those verses that specify a truth about the natural world, an understanding of empirical science precedes the understanding of the verse in question (Kārim Sayyid Ghanīm, pp. 61-62).

Contrarily, some have intended to invoke the epistemological position of the Qur'an, which is one of the reasons put forth by the proponents of scientific exegesis to prove the Qur'an's comprehensiveness, to derive the opposite conclusion. Sayyid Quṭb, for instance, maintains that since the meaning signified by Qur'anic verses is an indubitable truth, it would be wrong to identify it with any form of scientific knowledge, including those propositions that are merely theories and those that have ostensibly been verified as fact, for scientific knowledge is inevitably restricted to experience and the limited means available to the human being and as such is open to question. Thus it would be wrong to conflate these two modes of knowledge (Quṭb, vol. 1, p. 182). It is clear from this opinion, that the position of the Qur'an which is purely Divine and that of exegesis which is a human enterprise have not been distinctively separated and the rule pertinent to one is universally applied to the other.

Scientific exegesis has been criticised from yet another perspective. Shāṭibī, who is considered the strongest critic of scientific exegesis among former scholars, holds that the criterion for understanding the Qur'an is determined by the understanding of the original audience to whom the Qur'an was addressed during the Period of Revelation. Further, there is no indication of scientific exegesis in their words serving as sufficient evidence that the Qur'an does not include the empirical sciences (Shāṭibī, vol. 2, p. 389, vol. 3, p. 340). In recent times, this line of reasoning has been paraphrased by Amīn Khūlī, who formulated a number of principles as the basis for Qur'anic hermeneutics (Khūlī, pp. 293-294). According to Amīn Khūlī, when considering the historical context of revelation and the Qur'anic literature, two factors maybe be arrived at that must be taken into consideration when interpreting the Qur'an, and scientific exegesis fails to do so. These are, first, understanding the words in the Qur'an as they were understood in the Period of Revelation and, second, conforming our interpretation to what Muslims understood of the Qur'anic verses during the Period of Revelation (ibid.).

There is general consensus among Muslims and Qur'anic exegetes, in particular, that the words in the Qur'an should be understood in the meaning that they denoted in the Period of Revelation. One question, however, remains to be answered. Can new scientific findings serve as modifiers in determining and delimiting the precise meaning of a word in the Qur'an? Furthermore, the argument on the basis of Qur'an's literature warrants only that any interpretation inferred from a verse should correspond to the understanding of Muslims in the context of the Period of Revelation. As such, one's interpretation need not be limited to what was understood in the Period of Revelation. Rather, it must be such as to incorporate the meaning understood by the Muslims of the Period of Revelation (Qarḍāwī, p. 383; Sharīf, p. 671). For, to circumscribe the meaning of a verse exclusively to what the early Muslims understood would not only preclude scientific exegesis but would also bar any attempt at a more profound understanding of the Qur'an beyond what the early Muslims perceived. This would mean that all the exegetic works of the past fifteen centuries should be discarded as heretical.

Muḥammad 'Izza Darwaza, another critic of scientific exegesis, places the understanding of the Prophet as the Divinely appointed expositor of the Qur'an in lieu of the understanding of the Muslims of the Period of Revelation as the criterion for Qur'anic interpretation and so argues against scientific exegesis on the basis that it lacks support from the prophetic hadiths (vol. 2, p. 7). But while there is no doubt that the Prophet possessed the highest knowledge concerning the interpretation of the Qur'an, one may question whether he conveyed all his knowledge to his contemporary Muslims, especially as he underscored the necessity of speaking to people at the level of their comprehension.

Another question in this relation pertains to the implications of scientific exegesis. The proponents state that as scientific exegesis demonstrates the Qur'an's inimitability in the domain of science, it is a necessary approach to understanding the Qur'an. As they see it, to convince the people of the modern age—who are largely unfamiliar with the Arabic language and as such are incapable of grasping its literary inimitability—of the validity of the Qur'an and its timelessness, there is no choice but to have recourse to Qur'an's scientific inimitability (Ḥanafī Aḥmad, p. 17, Nawfal, pp. 6-7, 22-25; Jamīlī, p. 313; Sharī'atī Mazīnānī, p. LX).

The Qur'an's scientific inimitability is such an appealing subject to Muslim intellectuals that some have tried to solve this dilemma by differentiating between scientific exegesis and the scientific inimitability, claiming that the dispute concerns only the former, for all Muslims accept the Qur'an's scientific inimitability (Rūmī, vol. 2, pp. 600-601). It is for this reason that even certain critics of scientific exegesis have occasionally affirmed their belief in the Qur'an's scientific inimitability (Quṭb, vol. 5, p. 3095, vol. 6, p. 3878). Other critics of Qur'anic exegesis who are unwilling to concede Qur'an's scientific inimitability argue that to prove the Qur'an's timelessness, it would be sufficient to merely point to its compatibility with empirical science (Khūlī, p. 295; Shaltūt, p. 22; Dhahabī, vol. 2, pp. 539-540). It is unclear, however, how one could legitimately cite the Qur'an's scientific inimitability or its compatibility with empirical science without recourse to scientific exegesis, without illustrating how science relates to the Qur'an. For it is only through scientific exegesis that the necessary premises can be secured to arrive at the conclusions in question.

Some critics of scientific exegesis centre their criticisms on its negative ramifications. They point to the drastic transformations occurring in the realm of empirical science: What may have yesterday been thought of as scientific certainty may today be proven false. By engaging in scientific exegesis, we tie the fate of the Qur'an to the oscillations inherent in scientific development (Shaltūt, p. 21). A clear manifestation of this truth is Ṭanṭāwī's exegesis, which, despite its initial popularity, in a short time became obsolete. Having this negative consequence in mind, some scholars have postulated certain principles—such as conforming to the literal meaning and being mindful of the rules of the Arabic language that are necessary for a correct understanding of the text and identifying the instances where words are meant metaphorically rather than literally—in the hope that they would reduce such negative effects of any systematic exegesis, be it scientific or otherwise, to a minimum.

The advocates of scientific exegesis have also stressed the necessity of heading the above-mentioned conditions and have in unison with their critics condemned those who engage in Qur'anic interpretation without observing these conditions (Abū Ḥujr, pp. 210, 249; Dirāz, Arab. tr., p. 176). Some critics of scientific exegesis, however, go further to assert the insufficiency of taking merely the literal meaning into consideration, deeming it necessary that for a profound understanding of the meaning of the Qur'an, one should seek out its secrets and allegories (Ghazālī, 1412/1992, vol. 1, p. 383; Ḥanafī Aḥmad, pp. 5-6; Kārim Sayyid Ghanīm, p. 60).

In order to bestow greater integrity on scientific exegesis, some scholars have proposed that the scientific exeget should only consider the scientific facts to the exclusion of the scientific theories and hypotheses that are yet to be definitively verified. Since scientific facts are indubitable, they may serve as material for scientific exegesis (Abū Ḥujr, p. 209; Rūmī, vol. 2, p. 571; Dīyāb and Qurqūz, p. 12; Sharī'tī Mazīnānī, p. LXII; Qarḍāwī, p. 382). Other scholars, however, have examined this topic in greater detail by positing four possibilities as to the relation between the Qur'an and empirical science based on whether a verse or a scientific proposition is definitive or not: 1. that scientific fact should contradict a univocal verse; 2. that scientific fact should contradict an equivocal verse; 3. that a scientific theory should be opposed to a univocal verse; and 4.

that a scientific theory should be opposed to an equivocal verse. In relation to the first possibility, they propose abstaining from giving an opinion. With the second possibility, they maintain that the verse should be interpreted in accordance with scientific fact. And as regards the third and fourth possibilities, they affirm that the literal meaning of the verse should be upheld (Ṭabāṭabā'ī, vol. 17, p. 373; Kārim Sayyid Ghanīm, pp. 277-278).

Though the effort to give greater systematic consistency to scientific exegesis is admirable, it must be admitted that this exegesis is inevitably subject to change, which is a fundamental characteristic of human thought. This problem is further exacerbated by the fact that those who embark on scientific exegesis are inadequately acquainted with either empirical science or Qur'anic exegesis or both and are merely amateurs in both fields, and this has made scientific exegeses vulnerable to numerous deficiencies (Qarḍāwī, pp. 383-385; Kārim Sayyid Ghanīm, pp. 187-211).

Another reason that critics cite to dispute scientific exegesis is to point to the main purpose of the Qur'an and the role that the story of creation plays in this context, blaming the advocates of neglecting the Qur'an's main purpose. The critics assert that the Qur'an is the book of guidance, not science and that scientific exegesis fails to realise this (Shaltūt, p. 21; Khūlī, p. 298; Dhahabī, vol. 2, p. 540). A number of scholars explain that the Qur'an's purpose in depicting the story of creation is to draw the attention of its readers to the order inherent in nature indicating the existence of a wise creator and architect (Ḍayf, p. 10; Rūmī, vol. 2, p. 581; Dhahabī, vol. 2, p. 540). These scholars contend that to preoccupy ourselves with the intricate details of the natural phenomena would only distract us from the main purpose of assisting the addresses from ascertaining the intended rationale and wisdom of the Qu'ran (Ḍayf, p. 10). The proponents of scientific exegesis, however, reply that they too see the Qur'an as the book of guidance and the verses related to creation as premises for theological and moral arguments for proving the validity of the Qur'an (Rashīd Riḍā, vol. 1, pp. 17, 25; Rūmī, vol. 2, p. 571; Dīyāb and Qurqūz, p. 11; Ḥanafī Aḥmad, pp. 24, 34; Bāzargān, p. 330; Kārim Sayyid Ghanīm, p. 60). But in contrast to the critics, they are convinced that engaging in the scientific details of the verses on nature is not a superfluous endeavour and does not contradict the main purpose of the Qur'an.

Linguistic analysis informs yet another argument against scientific exegesis. This line of reasoning has been a matter of serious debate in the West concerning the relation between religion and science (Barbour, Pers. tr., pp. 277-287) but has been to a lesser extent explored in connection with Qur'anic exegesis. Philosophers who have taken up linguistic analysis conclude that language is a means that, depending on the field in which it is employed, takes on various functions. From this perspective, the language that the Qur'an employs in describing nature is that of ordinary laypeople, hence the abundance of amphibology, analogy, and metaphor in Qur'anic literature. This distinguishes it from scientific language. As these two languages are different, the two fields of empirical science and Qur'anic exegesis are independent from each other, the distinction leaves Qur'anic exegesis immune from the changes in science; nonetheless, it deprives the former of the latter's benefits.

12. MODERN APPROACHES TO EXEGESIS OF THE QUR'AN

Department of Qur'an and Ḥadīth

The encounter of the Muslim world with the West in modern history, far from impeding the progress of the discipline of Qur'anic exegesis, has added impetus to it. Qur'anic exegetes have thus developed novel approaches and methods in the field of the Qur'anic sciences in addition to pursuing traditional methods and approaches. This has led to the authorship of works in the same vein as those of previous eras or to the revision of earlier exegeses. This modern revival is rooted in the progressive spirit pervading the modern world of Islam and aspires to the same values cherished by the modern Muslim intelligentsia — such as Islamic solidarity in the face of Western imperialism, dispelling popular superstitions, restoring Islam to its pristine origins, and reconciling Islamic doctrine with science and new scientific discoveries ('Ināyat, p. 11). As far as motives are concerned, the modern trend is not drastically different from that of previous eras. It is, rather, distinguished in its new-found purposes, themes, and methods.

What ushered the Qur'an into centre stage in the studies of progressive Muslim scholars, especially in the Sunnī school, was the belief that the Qur'an outweighed the other sources of Islamic thought—e.g., hadith, *qīyās* (analogy), and *ijmā'* (consensus)—(idid., p. 25). Despite differences and disparities, generally speaking modern exegetic studies share three common elements: presenting a reasonable exposition, discarding myths and superstitions surrounding the Qur'an, and formulating on a rational basis the theoretical principles of Islam and the principles corresponding to or justified by the Qur'an (Encyclopedia of Religion, vol. 14, p. 242). What aided and legitimised the efforts of these scholars, who inaugurated the modern trend in exegetic studies, was their utilising of method commonly practised by the jurisprudents. This constitutes meticulous scrutiny of apocryphal hadiths—such as the traditions of biblical origin (*isrā'īlīyyāt*), which had found their way into previous Qur'anic exegeses. To this end, they also made use of new methods in textual analysis of historical and literary texts, which ultimately led to the repudiation of many dubious reports ('Ināyat, p. 27).

The body of exegetic studies produced in recent times may be classified into two groups: 1. exegeses that treat of the entire Qur'an or parts of it with a new approach; 2. texts, treatises, or articles that merely propose a new exegetic method without actually applying it in interpreting the Qur'an. The second group, though less appealing than the first, is as significant in signifying a new method and in the results that they may entail (Nayfar, p. 27). The first group comprises such divergent approaches as the Salafī, the rationalist-reformist, and the progressive.

The Salafī approach in Qur'anic exegesis is based on the opinions of traditional exegetes, the corpus of reported hadiths, and the tradition of the pious predecessors. Although, it is in a sense the continuation of the classic exegetic tradition (Muḥtasib, p. 41), its interpretations of the Qur'an and the

Prophetic traditions in general differ from those of the traditional exegetic method. The fundamental principle of this approach is that it recognises adherence to the Prophetic traditions as guaranteeing the cultural and intellectual unity of the Muslims and as a means of defence against the onslaught of foreign cultures (Nayfar, p. 27).

The most prominent Qur'anic exegetes of this persuasion are;

1. Shanqīṭī (d. 1352 AHS/1973-1974), Mauritanian scholar and exegete and author of the incomplete Qur'anic exegesis *Aḍwā' al-Bayān fī Īḍāḥ al-Qur'an*;

2. 'Abd al-Raḥmān ibn Nāṣir Āl Saʿdī al-Nāṣirī (d. 1336 AHS/1957-1958), Saudi jurisprudent and author of *Taysīr al-Karīm al-Raḥmān fī Tafsīr Kalām al-Mannān*;

3. Muḥammad Ṭāhir ibn 'Āshūr (d. 1352 AHS/1973-1974), famous Tunisian jurisprudent and reformist and author of *al-Taḥrīr wa al-Tanwīr* in thirty volumes, which is the most important Qur'anic exegesis produced in the western hemisphere of the Muslim world (ibid., p. 35);

4. Muḥammad 'Alī Ṣābūnī, author of *Rawā'iʿ al-Bayān fī Tafsīr Āyāt al-Aḥkām fī al-Qur'an*. In Iran and the Shī'a world, two Qur'anic exegetes may be mentioned as belonging to the Salafī denomination: Muḥammad Ḥasan Sharī'at Sangelajī (d. 1322 AHS/1943-1944), author of *Kilīd-i Fahm-i Qur'an* and Yūsuf Shi'ār (d. 1352 AHS/1973-1974), author of *Tafsīr-i Āyāt-i Mushkil-i Qur'an*.

The rationalist-reformist approach, which is actually an offshoot of the Salafī denomination (ibid., p. 41), is designated as a rationalist school of thought for its acknowledgement of reason as a credible source for Qur'anic exegesis (Rūmī, vol. 2, p. 730). The rationalist-reformist approach places reason on a par with Revelation, in fact considering Revelation as complementing reason. For this reason, it evaluates Islamic doctrine on the basis of rational principles and the contributions of modern Western civilisation, intending thereby to reduce the gap between Western and Islamic civilisations (Rūmī, vol. 1, pp. 809-810). The founder of this school of thought was Muḥammad 'Abduh (d. 1323/1905) who was strongly influenced by the reformist Sayyid Jamāl al-Dīn Asadābādī, a critic of the predominant tendency among Qur'anic exegetes in contenting themselves with the literal meaning of the verses of the Qur'an, such as the meaning of the preposition *bi* in *bi-'sm-i 'llāh* (Makhzūmī, p. 160).

'Abduh taught Qur'anic exegesis, starting from the beginning of the Qur'an and up to 4:125 (Rashīd Riḍā, vol. 1, p. 14). He also produced and published separate exegeses of the last part (*juz'*) of the Qur'an and of Sura al-'Aṣr (103). His main purpose in engaging in Qur'anic exegesis was to bring to light issues that prior exegetes had neglected (Rashīd Riḍā, vol. 1, pp. 14-15). He proclaimed that the earlier exegeses were mainly concerned with the Qur'an's literary and rhetorical aspects and as such failed to reveal the true spirit of the Qur'an, thus depriving people of a correct understanding of the Qur'an (ibid., pp. 26-27). 'Abduh based his exegetic views on his reformist principles, and since he believed in the precedence of reason when it happened to contradict hadith ('Abduh, 1976, p. 45), he tended to dismiss transmitted interpretation (Rashīd Riḍā, vol. 1, pp. 9-10). It was specifically due to this rationalistic tendency that he never consulted former exegeses of the Qur'an and strove to offer interpretations of such Qur'anic terms as angel, Satan (ibid., pp. 269, 281-282), and wizardry ('Abduh, 1973, vol. 5, p. 567, 'Abd al-Ghaffār 'Abd al-Raḥīm, pp. 255-258) and such verses as *[Did He not] send against them flocks of birds, pelting them with stones of shale* (105:3-4; 'Abduh, 1973, vol. 5, pp. 527-529) that he thought were more palatable to reason. While affirming the thematic unity of verses of the Qur'an (ibid., vol. 2, p. 11), he maintained the necessity of the disciplines of Arabic grammar and rhetoric in correctly inferring the meaning intended by God (Rashīd Riḍā, vol. 1, p. 22). Moreover, 'Abduh emphasised the importance of examining the words of the Qur'an in their historical context and as they were used at the time of revelation (idib., vol. 1, pp. 21-22).

'Abduh's approach was followed by, among others, the following: 1. Muḥammad Rashīd Riḍā (d. 1345/1935), 'Abduh's most prominent student and author of the incomplete exegesis *al-Manār*, which closely resembles the teacher's rationalist approach (Dhahabī, vol. 2, p. 551), barring certain exceptions (e.g. the validity of invoking authentic hadiths, which 'Abduh denied) as expounded in the introduction to the exegesis (vol,1 p.16); 2. Muḥammad Jamāl al-Dīn Qāsimī (d. 1333/1920), author of the Qur'anic exegesis *Maḥāsin al-Ta'wīl*; 3. Muḥammad Muṣṭafā al-Marāghī (d. 1364/1951), a student of 'Abduh; 4. Muḥammad 'Izza Darwaza (d. 1363 AHS/1983), author of the Qur'anic exegesis *al-Tafsīr al-Ḥadīth*, which follows the verses of the Qur'an in their chronological occasions of revelation; 5. 'Abd al-Ḥamīd ibn Bādīs (d. 1359/1947), an Algerian reformist intellectual and a leader of the resistance movement fighting French colonialism ('Abd al-Mun'im Namr, p. 137), whose exegetic writings have been partially collected and published under the title of *Majālis al-Tadhkīr min Kalām al-Ḥakīm al-Khabīr*; 6. Aḥmad Muṣṭafā al-Marāghī (d. 1372/1958.), author of *Tafsīr al-Marāghī*; 7. 'Abd al-'Azīz Jāwīsh, author of *Asrār al-Qur'an*; 8. 'Abd al-Karīm Khaṭīb, author of *al-Tafsīr al-Qur'anī li-'l-Qur'an*; and finally 9. 'Abd al-Qādir Maghribī (d. 1375/1961.), whose only surviving piece of Qur'anic exegesis is an exegesis of part twenty nine of the Qur'an (Rūmī, vol. 1, p. 207). One may also name Abū al-Kalām Āzād (d. 1379/1958), Indian scholar and a supporter of Gandhi in fighting for independence from British rule, who wrote *Tarjumān al-Qur'an* in Urdu, influenced by the teachings of 'Abduh (Āzād Fārūqī, pp. 47-70).

At the time, when Islamic countries were becoming increasingly Westernised, political, social, and cultural opposition gained ground on a large scale in the Muslim world, leading to the formation of numerous Muslim resistance groups. A central element unifying these various groups was embracing the Qur'an as the fulcrum and declaring that all Muslims should reinstate their belief in the Qur'an and struggle in whatever way possible to aid the implementation of its injunctions. This movement may be concisely described as an engagement in Qur'anic interpretation to effect change. Ḥasan al-Bannā', the founder of the Muslim Brotherhood, was one of the prominent figures who wrote a number of works on Qur'anic exegesis, including *Risālatān fī al-Tafsīr, Sūra al-Fātiḥa* and *Maqāṣid Sūra al-Baqara* (Khurramshāhī, p. 29).

The most eminent personage, however, in this exegetic movement is Sayyid Quṭb (d. 1966), a member of the Muslim Brotherhood. He wrote several works of Qur'anic exegesis, the most notable being *al-Tafsīr fī Ẓilāl al-Qur'an*. Though in part influenced by the rationalist-reformist approach represented by *al-Manār*, Sayyid Quṭb disagreed on numerous points, such as *al-Manār*'s rationalist interpretation of such concepts as angel and Satan, asserting instead that we must believe in such concepts faithfully and without question (e.g. Quṭb, vol. 4, pp. 30-31, vol. 8, pp. 670-671). Sayyid Quṭb is of the conviction that the exegete should refrain from relying on his preconceived rationalist assumptions in interpreting the Qur'an (vol. 8, p. 671). Sayyid Quṭb posits that the suras of the Qur'an possess one theme, which he designates as the "fulcrum" (*miḥwar*, e.g. vol. 1, p. 23, vol. 2, p. 623, vol. 5, p. 121). The Qur'an, in his view, is a literary text that the exegete must decipher, but this can be achieved only if one experiences the Qur'an on a personal level and feels oneself addressed by it in the way that the Muslims at the Period of Revelation were. As such, only those who possess the motivation to effect change are capable of understanding the Qur'an (Nayfar, pp. 64-65). In other words, Sayyid Quṭb is a salafī who views the Islamic jihad of the early Muslims rather than their cultural heritage as his inspiration (ibid.).

In Iran and, in general, amongst the Shī'a, the most esteemed exegete vocal in his opposition to imperialist tyranny and motivated by a reformist mindset was Sayyid Maḥmūd Ṭāliqānī (d. 1358 AHS/1979). His Qur'anic exegesis, *Partuwī az Qur'an*, extend to 4:28 and also includes the entire thirtieth part of the Qur'an. His purpose in writing this exegesis, which was in the main the fruit of his reflections during his time in prison and in exile, was to revive the teachings of the Qur'an and to re-establish it as a basis for intellectual exchange and social activism (Ṭāliqānī, vol. 1, p. 13). This was also the motivation that compelled Abū al-Aʿlā Mawdūdī (d. 1358 AHS/1979), the famous Pakistani intellectual and author, to write the Qur'anic exegesis *Tafhīm al-Qur'an* in Urdu.

Among the great variety of Qur'anic exegeses written in recent times in the Muslim world are some that elude any attempt to categorise them under a single classification. These exegeses, which are inevitably influenced by the modern milieu, have recourse to all the above-mentioned approaches without confining themselves in a single framework. In this relation, one may refer to the works of Maḥmūd Shaltūt (d. 1963) in the Sunnī world, the late grand mufti of Egypt, such as his *Ilā al-Qur'an al-Karīm, Min Hudā al-Qur'an*, and *Tafsīr al-Qur'an al-Karīm*. In the Shīʿa world, one may point to *Tafsīr Nuwīn* by Muḥammad Taqī Sharīʿatī, certain works by Mahdī Bāzargān, *Tafsīr-i Nimūna* (published under the supervision of Nāṣir Makārim Shīrāzī), and *al-Tafsīr al-Kāshif* by Muḥammad Jawād Mughnīya as some of the works belonging to this category. Unrivalled, however, in the Shīʿa world in this regard is *Tafsīr al-Mīzān* by Sayyid Muḥammad Ḥusayn Ṭabāṭabā'ī. The latter employs the method of contextual interpretation (*tafsīr al-qur'an bi-'l-qur'an*) but in addition also taps into a vast reservoir of both early and recent literature encompassing literary works, Qur'anic exegeses, corpus of hadith, and theological texts, and, while mindful of the intellectual and social dilemmas of modern times, has steered clear of the pitfall of scientism (Khurramshāhī, pp. 115-132).

As to the second category of contemporary exegeses of the Qur'an, which offer a methodology for interpretation and an analysis of the Qur'an, we may point to the literary and interpretive (*ta'wīlī*) approaches and the independent approaches of such figures as Ḥasan Ḥanafī and Muḥammad Shuḥrūr.

The literary approach to interpreting the Qur'an, which is also known as the rhetorical approach, views the Qur'an from a purely literary perspective. This approach is epitomised by *al-Manār*, which lays emphasis on this aspect of the Qur'an (Nayfar, p. 79). Though the literary aspect of the Qur'an was also a main focus in traditional exegeses, but it was so as a means of proving the Qur'an's inimitable nature. In the contemporary approach, however, the literary aspect is studied for its own sake and as a final goal (Rūmī, vol. 3, pp. 881-882) and without attention to any other concern (Khūlī, p. 230). Those who take this approach, like those who endorse the approach epitomised by *al-Manār*, agree that the main purpose in interpreting the Qur'an is to shed light on its function as Divine guidance but at the same time maintain that the exegete must first examine its Arabic literature (Khūlī, p. 229; Shukrī Muḥammad ʿĪyād, pp. 6-7). The proponents of this approach reduce the question of the Qur'an's inimitability to a rhetorical and literary concern confined within the framework of the scripture. Furthermore, they deem it necessary that the exegete should treat of the meaning of the Qur'an, its content, historical context, and psychological and sociological aspects in relation to the reality.

The founder of this approach is Amīn Khūlī, renowned Egyptian author and scholar (d. 1345 AHS/1966). He propounded his views in this relation in *Minhāj al-Tajdīd fī al-Naḥw wa al-Balāgha wa al-Tafsīr wa al-Adab* (published 1951) and in an article entitled "Al-Tafsīr," which he contributed to the encyclopedia *Dāʾirat al-Maʿārif al-Islāmiyya* (vol. 9, pp. 411-438). The literary interpretation he espouses comprises two stages. In the first stage, the verses of the Qur'an are classified thematically so as to shed light on the concepts considered by the Qur'an. In the second stage, he examines the historical origins of the verses and the constituent words, then the external elements weighing on the text, i.e., place of revelation and the lifestyle and culture of the early Muslims who were directly addressed by the Qur'an

(Khūlī, p. 235), and finally the Qur'anic text is analysed in view of its vocabulary, the various elements leading to changes in meaning, and the compound structure of the sentences. This is how Khūlī proposed to study the style and methodology of the verses of the Qur'an (ibid., pp. 237-239). Amīn Khūlī's pupil and spouse, 'Ā'isha 'Abd al-Raḥmān bint al-Shāṭī (d. 1998), produced several works in this vein, the most prominent being *al-Tafsīr al-Bayānī li-'l-Qur'an al-Karīm*, which pursues the method of literary interpretation.

Muḥammad Aḥmad Khalaf Allāh (d. 1998), another pupil of Amīn Khūlī, wrote *al-Fann al-Qaṣaṣī fī al-Qur'an al-Karīm*, his doctoral dissertation, which was influenced by the teachings of his mentor. By applying Khūlī's method to the narratives of the Qur'an, he sought to present a reasonable exposition of them. In his view, the stories articulated in the Qur'an are moral parables couched in allegory and as such are not historical accounts (Muḥammad Aḥmad Khalaf Allāh, p. 22). Thus, in order to resolve the problem of traditions of biblical origin (*Isrā'īliyyāt*) with the various explanations offered in their justification and to grasp the main purpose of the stories of the Qur'an, he maintained that we must extricate them of the constraints of historicity (ibid., p. 73).

Shukrī Muḥammad 'Iyād (1921-), another pupil of Amīn Khūlī, pinned *Yawm al-Dīn wa al-Ḥisāb: min Waṣf al-Qur'an li-Yawm al-Dīn wa Yawm al-Ḥisāb*, in which he applied his teacher's method to the verses concerning the Day of Judgment.

The last contemporary approach to the interpretation of the Qur'an discussed here is termed the interpretive (*ta'wīlī*) approach, which came into existence and flourished in the first two decades of the fifteenth century (1979-1999). This approach, on the one hand, continues the method developed in the works of Amīn Khūlī and his pupils and the interpretive methods of past centuries. But on the other hand, it seeks to take advantage of the intellectual developments of the West (Nayfar, p. 91). Hence, *ta'wīlī* differs drastically from its traditional sense. In the contemporary sense, it represents an interplay between the text and the reader (ibid., p. 92). In essence, this approach interprets the Qur'an as a cultural phenomenon that is able to be readjusted to accommodate the findings of modern science (ibid.). The most outstanding advocates of this approach are as follows: 1. Muḥammad Arkūn (1928-), author of a number of works, including *Qirā'āt al-Qur'an wa al-Fikr al-Islāmī: Qirā'a 'Ilmiyya*; 2. Naṣr Ḥāmid Abū Zayd (1943-), author of such works as *al-Ittijāh al-'Aqlī fī al-Tafsīr, Mafhūm al-Naṣṣ, Ishkālīyyāt al-Qirā'a wa Āliyyāt al-Ta'wīl wa al-Naṣṣ*, and *al-Sulṭa*; 3. and to a lesser degree, Faḍl al-Raḥmān (d. 1988), who wrote several works on this theme, such as *Maḍāmīn al-Qur'an* (Nayfar, pp. 91-104).

Mention should also be made of two other individuals who sought to introduce a novel approach to the interpretation of the Qur'an. Firstly, there is Ḥasan Ḥanafī who formulated his fundamental principles in his doctoral dissertation entitled "Exegetic Methods" and in parts of his book, *al-Turāth wa al-Tajdīd*. In his works, he criticises the methodology of the "orientalists" (Ḥasan Ḥanafī, 1412/1992, p. 86) and also that of Muslim scholars who study the Islamic heritage (ibid., p. 96) to affirm the necessity of revising the methods in question. He proposes a new approach that may be dubbed the "social method" in interpreting the Qur'an (Ḥasan Ḥanafī 1419/1999, p. 174). According to this method, only those parts of the Qur'an that cater to the real needs of the modern society ought to be interpreted (ibid., p. 175). Secondly, there is Muḥammad Shuḥrūr, the Syrian academic. In his book, *al-Kitāb wa al-Qur'an: Qirā'a Mu'āṣira* (Beirut: 2000), he undertakes to offer a new scheme for reading and interpreting the Qur'an.

Generally speaking, the endeavours of contemporary Muslim exegetes, share three elements, regardless of which of the two denominations they belong to: 1. an effort to reach out to a larger audience for Qur'anic interpretation due to the advancement of modern civil institutions and education; 2. an expansion of the practice of Qur'anic exegesis so that the traditional centres are no longer the exclusive domains in which exegetic works are produced (one may point to India, Pakistan, Morocco, and Southeast Asia as new foci wherein Qur'anic exegesis flourishes); 3. attention to problems that hitherto went largely neglected, such as moral, social, and economic problems with which modern societies grapple (Oxford Encyclopedia of the Modern Islamic World, vol. 4, p. 174; for a quick glimpse at the extent that such topics are of concern in contemporary exegeses of the Qur'an. It may suffice to gloss over the thematic index of *Tafsīr al-Mīzān* entitled *Dalīl al-Mīzān* and that of *Tafsīr-i Nimūna* and *Tafsīr-i Rāhnamā*, which cover a fairly exhaustive list of the topics treated by contemporary exegetes).

13. EXEGETIC STUDIES IN THE MUSLIM WORLD

Mihrdād 'Abbāsī

After being established by exegetes as a standard practice in the exposition and explanation of the meaning of the verses of the Qur'an, Muslim scholars came to study Qur'anic exegesis as an independent branch of learning with peculiar principles, guidelines, and approaches. These scholars have, furthermore, sought to introduce and evaluate Qur'anic exegetes and the exegeses they have provided, from the beginning of this discipline to the present time. The works Muslim scholars have produced to this end fall into three categories.

1. The first category comprises the works dealing with the science of Qur'anic exegesis and the explication of its principles and guidelines. The authors who have written such works expound their views on the principles necessary for a correct exposition of the Qur'an and the prerequisites and requirements needed to achieve such exposition without referring to particular exegetes or methods of exegesis. These works pursue the study of

the principles and guidelines of the discipline.

The study of the principles of Qur'anic exegesis concerns the guidelines and premises on which the science of Qur'anic exegesis is based, and as such its relation to *tafsīr* is comparable to that of principles of jurisprudence (*uṣūl al-fiqh*) to jurisprudence (*fiqh*) or that of *naḥw* (syntax) to Arabic literature (Rūmī, p. 11; Ṣabbāgh, p. 10; Sabt, p. 33). Some scholars equate the study of the principles of exegesis with the broader term of "Qur'anic sciences," deeming it to encompass all the sciences suggested by the latter (Sabt, p. 33; 'Ubayd, p. 28), but it seems that a more accurate understanding would be to consider the study of the principles of exegesis as only one of the branches of the Qur'anic sciences, though it is indeed one of the most important and outstanding ones (Rūmī, p. 12; 'Ubayd, pp. 28-29). It is for this reason that the texts on the Qur'anic sciences invariably include a discussion of at least some of the principles of Qur'anic exegesis (see below).

As various scholars hold diverging views regarding this study, it is hard to delimit strictly the topics that may be treated in it (Ṭayyār, p. 14). There are, however, certain topics that are by consensus included in this branch of study, which are as follows: the definition of *tafsīr* and how it differs from *ta'wīl* and *tarjama*, the permissibility of engaging in *tafsīr*, what constitutes *tafsīr bi al-ra'y*, the various genres of *tafsīr*, leading to disagreement in interpreting a verse, the necessary sciences that an exegete must be equipped with, the conditions that an exegete must meet, etc. (ibid., pp. 14-15). But there is not a single text that deals with these principles in an exhaustive manner (ibid., p. 12). The most important works produced in this regard are those that treat exclusively of these principles, which generally include *uṣūl tafsīr* or *qawā'id tafsīr* in their titles.

Al-Iksīr fī 'Ilm al-Tafsīr (Cairo: 1977) by Ṭawfī Sulaymn Ṣarṣarī Baghdādī (d. 716/1316-1317) is the earliest work written dealing independently with the science of exegesis. Ṣabbāgh (p. 274) is of the opinion that the original name of the book was *al-Iksīr fī*

Qawā'id al-Tafsīr, imputing the editors for the change in title. In this work, Baghdādī studies merely the science of Arabic rhetoric and how it plays out in the Qur'an, and as such this book fails to merit inclusion among the books dealing with the principles of exegesis as defined above. Thus, the first genuine work of this genre is Ibn Taymiyya's *Muqaddima fī Uṣūl al-Tafsīr*. The author says that he wrote this short treatise at the behest of a friend and so that it may help Muslims in better understanding God's Word. He claims to have included therein the general principles that are conducive to a correct understanding of the Qur'an and the science of exegesis and that may help in distinguishing between the true and the false opinions related thereto (Ibn Taymiyya, p. 7). It was the grand mufti of Demascene Ḥanbalīs, rather than Ibn Taymiyya himself, who gave the book its title and published it in 1355/1936-1937 (Ṭayyār, p. 12).

Al-Taysīr fī Qawā'id 'Ilm al-Tafsīr (Damascus: 1990) by Muḥammad ibn Sulaymān Kāfiyajī (d. 879/1474-1475) is another work primarily concerning the Qur'anic sciences (Sabt, p. 44).

A later work that also merits mention is *Al-Fawz al-Kabīr fī Uṣūl al-Tafsīr* (Beirut and Damascus: 1989) by Shāh Walī Allāh Dihlawī (d. 1176/1762-1763). The author's purpose in writing this work was to make accessible in the form of certain principles the discoveries he made in the way of understanding the Qur'an and by way of Divine revelation to those who expend much time reading the conventional works of Qur'anic exegesis (Shāh Walī Allāh Dihlawī, p. 2). To this end, he introduced five sciences inherent in the Qur'an, the knowledge of which would facilitate a better comprehension of the Qur'an.

In his *Tawshīḥ al-Tafsīr fī Qawā'id al-Tafsīr wa al-Ta'wīl* (Qum: 1411/1990-1991), the Shī'a scholar Muḥammad ibn Sulaymān Tunikābunī (d. 1302/1884-1885), after articulating certain preliminary points, produces certain principles that, he claims, an exegete must consider when interpreting the verses of the Qur'an.

In *al-Qawā'id al-Ḥisān li-Tafsīr al-Qur'an* (Riyadh: 1993), 'Abd al-Raḥmān ibn Nāṣir Sa'dī (fl. 1365/1946) postulates seventy principles for Qur'anic exegesis. In addition to expounding each principle, he illustrates numerous instances for each from the Qur'an.

A list of some contemporary works in this field is as follows: 1. *Uṣūl al-Tafsīr wa Qawāʿiduh* (Beirut: 1986) by Khālid ʿAbd al-Raḥmān ʿAkk; 2. *Buḥūth fī Uṣūl al-Tafsīr wa Manāhijih* (Riyadh: 1419/1998-1999) by Fahd ibn ʿAbd al-Raḥmān ibn Sulaymān Rūmī; 3. *Fuṣūl fī Uṣūl al-Tafsīr* (Riyadh: 1413/1992-1993) by Musāʿid ibn Sulaymān Ṭayyār; 4. *Qawāʿid al-Tafsīr Jamʿan wa Dirāsatan* (Egypt: 1421/2000-2001) by Khālid ibn ʿUthmān Sabt; 5. *Rawishshināsī-yi Tafsīr-i Qurʾan* (Tehran: 1379 AHS/2000-2001) by ʿAlī Akbar Bābāʾī, et al. (for further sources on this topic, see *Dānishnāma-yi Qurʾan wa Qurʾanpazhūhī*, vol. 2, pp. 1808-1809; Āshūrī, *Bayyināt*, vol. 1, no. 3, pp. 162-169, no. 4, pp. 170-177, vol. 2, no. 1, pp. 168-173; Zarkashī, vol. 2, pp. 276-277, n.)

In addition to the independent works written in this field, we may also point to the introductions contemporary and early exegetes have written to their Qur'anic exegeses, which may be viewed as examinations of the principles of exegesis. In this relation, one may mention Ṭabarī (vol. 1, pp. 2-36), Ibn ʿAṭiyya (vol. 1, pp. 1-47), Quṭrubī (vol. 1, pp. 4-107), Abū Ḥayyān (vol. 1, pp. 2-13), Ibn Kathīr (vol. 1, pp. 5-14), Fayḍ Kāshānī (vol. 1, pp. 15-78), and Ālūsī (vol. 1, pp. 2-33) as some of the exegetes who have included such introductions in their works. (For names of other exegetes, see *ʿUlūm al-Qurʾan ʿind al-Mufassirīn*, vol. 3, pp. 169-368; Zarkashī, vol. 2, pp. 276-277).

Some exegetes, however, have written on the principles of Qur'anic exegesis at greater lengths than others. The earliest example of such an extensive introduction to a Qur'anic exegesis belongs to Rāghib Iṣfahānī, the author of *Jāmiʿ al-Tafāsīr* (Kuwait, 1984). In expressing his purpose in writing the introduction, he states (p. 9) that he intends it as an elucidation of and expansion on the points mentioned in brief by the Companions, Successors, and other great figures.

Jamāl al-Dīn Qāsimī has devoted the first volume of his exegesis on the Qur'an, *Maḥāsin al-Taʾwīl*, to this purpose. In it he details eleven exegetic principles along with other general points concerning Qur'anic exegesis. He has designated this volume by the title *Tamhīd Khaṭīr fī Qawā'id al-Tafsīr* (vol. 1, pp. 7-349). In the same vein, Ibn 'Āshūr (vol. 1, pp. 10-130) introduces his book with ten preliminary sections in which he elucidates in depth his exegetic principles. Also, the texts on Qur'anic sciences include certain discussions related to the principles and guidelines of Qur'anic exegesis (e.g. Zarkashī, vol. 2, pp. 283-348; Suyūṭī, vol. 4, pp. 192-230; Zurqānī, vol. 2, pp. 3-106).

2. The second category of works in this relation are the *ṭabaqāt*, a general term for books that typically index in chronological or alphabetical order the successive generations of authors and their works in a certain field, and the *ma'ājim*, i.e., biographical dictionaries, which undertake to introduce the exegetes and their works in a summary fashion. Though there are numerous works in the form of *ṭabaqāt* dedicated to jurisprudents, scholars of hadith, poets, and others (Ṭāshkūprīzāda, vol. 1, pp. 263-266; Ḥājī Khalīfa, vol. 2, col.s 1095-1108; Āqā Buzurg Ṭihrānī, vol. 15, pp. 145-153), and in spite of Ṭāshkūprīzāda's study on numerous extensive *ṭabaqāt* pertaining to exegetes (vol. 1, p. 263), there are no such works before the ninth/fitfeeth century. In fact, it was the lack of such a work that compelled Suyūṭī to compile his *Ṭabaqāt al-Mufassirīn* (Suyūṭī, 1960, p. 2).

Suyūṭī's intention was to write an exhaustive work cataloguing all the exegets of the Qur'an, including the Companions, the Successors, and the subsequent generations from all denominations and persuasions. His work, however, was cut short by his death, and he succeeded in treating of only 139 exegets (Suyūṭī, 1960, p. 43; Dāwūdī, vol. 1, the publisher's preface, p. II). Suyūṭī opens the book with an introduction on the various exegetic persuasions and the exegets adhering to them, enumerating four general persuasions. Suyūṭī ordered his book alphabetically. After providing the personal information regarding each exeget, he then names his teachers and students and specifies his works.

The incompleteness of Suyūṭī's work led his student, Muḥammad ibn 'Alī ibn Aḥmad Dāwūdī (d. 945/1538-1539), to write a book using the same title as that of his teacher. This work, completed in 941/1534-1535 (vol. 2, p. 386), makes use of numerous sources and quotes abundantly from *ṭabaqāt, tarājim*, and historical texts. Like his teacher, he has arranged this work in alphabetical order, examining therein seven hundred and four renowned exegetes, from the incipient phase of the discipline of Qur'anic exegesis to the turn of the tenth/sixteenth century. This work is in two volumes and generally contains better detailed comments than Suyūṭī's. Dāwūdī's book is acknowledged as the best text of its kind (Ḥājī Khalīfa, vol. 2, col. 1107; Nuwayhiḍ, vol. 1, p. IV).

Ḥājī Khalīfa (vol. 2, col. 1107) and Ismā'īl Baghdādī (vol. 1, col. 393) mention a certain Abū Sa'īd Kūzakunānī (d. 980/1572-1573; Kūzakunān is an area near Tabrīz) as the author of a work similar in title or content to Dāwūdī's. There is no indication, however, as to whether this book has survived.

About a century after Dāwūdī, Aḥmad ibn Muḥammad Adnawī (fl. 1092) compiled a *Ṭabaqāt al-Mufassirīn* that contained the accounts of six hundred and thirty eight exegets. He assigned each chapter of his book to the exegets of one century, studying them in chronological order, starting with the formative period of Islam and going up to the eleventh/seventeenth century, thereby diverging from the alphabetical arrangement employed by Suyūṭī and Dāwūdī. In examining each exeget, Adnawī first offers the usual personal details sought in such a context and then considers the exeget's works, especially those related to Qur'anic exegesis. In addition to being a reliable source of information concerning how the science of Qur'anic exegesis evolved over time, it helps us in distinguishing each generation of exegets from their predecessors and students (Adnawī, Khazī's introduction, pp. 7-8). The author finished this work toward the end of 1095/1683-1684. Among his sources, he mentions a book entitled *Mukhtaṣar Ṭabaqāt al-Mufassirīn* by Bayḍāwī, which is now lost.

In time and as more and more exegetes produced Qur'anic exegeses, the latter three works became obsolete. This fact motivated 'Ādil Nuwayhiḍ, contemporary Lebanese scholar, to author *Mu'jam al-Mufassirīn min Ṣadr al-Islām ḥattā al-'Aṣr al-Ḥāḍir*. This two-volume work contains the accounts of nearly two thousand exegetes, spanning from the early history of Islam to the present time. Nuwayhiḍ has opted for the alphabetical order, and where there are more than one entry competing for the same alphabetical slot, he determines the order based on the date of death. In addition to the usual details that he furnishes in keeping with his predecessors, he specifies whether the exegesis in question has been published or remains in manuscript form (Nuwayhiḍ, vol. 1, pp. VII-X).

Another work dealing with Qur'anic exegesis that uses the dictionary (*mu'jam*) format is *al-Mufassirūn Ḥayātuhum wa Manhajuhum* by Muḥammad 'Alī Ayāzī. This work, in lieu of the names of exegetes, lists the names of the Qur'anic exegeses in alphabetical order. In each entry, Ayāzī first comments on the author and the exegesis and after providing some general points concerning the scholarly background and works of the author analyses meticulously the exegesis and its methodology by citing excerpts from it. One of the distinctions of this book is its mention of the works written regarding a particular exegesis or exegete. Ayāzī's work covers a hundred and twenty one renowned exegeses of the Qur'an in Arabic and Persian from both the Shī'a and the Sunnī schools.

Another work is the five-volume *Ṭabaqāt Mufassirān Shī'a* by 'Abd al-Raḥīm 'Aqīqī Bakhshāyishī, which deals exclusively with the Shī'a school, introducing in brief close to two thousand Qur'anic exegetes and scholars ('Aqīqī Bakhshāyishī, vol. 5, p. 457; for further details about this work, see Raḥīm Qāsimī, pp. 20-29).

Another form of studies on Qur'anic exegeses that may be placed within this category comprises those works related to the history of Qur'anic exegesis and its trajectory of development. Some examples of this form are (1) *Tārīkh al-Tafsīr* (Maṭba'a

al-Majma' al-'Ilmī al-'Irāqī: 1966) by Shaykh Qāsim Qaysī;
(2) *Tārīkh al-Qur'an wa al-Tafsīr* (Egypt: 1972) by 'Abd Allāh
Maḥmūd Shaḥāta; (3) and *Tārīkh Tafsīr Qur'an Karīm* (Tehran:
1371 AHS/1992-1993) by Ḥabīb Allāh Jalālīyān (for further details
on related sources, see *Dānishnāma-yi Qur'an wa Qur'an Pazhūhī*,
vol. 2, p. 1810).

The above-mentioned works are those that deal explicitly
and independently with Qur'anic exegets, their works, and
the history of this discipline. One may, however, come upon
helpful information in this relation in reading other books
as well. Ḥājī Khalīfa (vol. 1, col.s 427-462), after presenting an
introduction to the science of Qur'anic exegesis, considers the
exegets from among the Companions and the Successors and
their works. He elaborates on the numerous exegetic persuasions
and enumerates hundreds of Qur'anic exegeses, selecting only a
few for more detailed explanation.

Āqā Buzurg Ṭihrānī (vol. 4, pp. 231-346) enumerates three
hundred and fifty Shī'a Qur'anic exegeses, only a few of which
are complete exegeses of the Qur'an, some being so short as to
treat of only a single verse. Muḥsin Amīn 'Āmilī's (vol. 1, pp.
125-127) also examines Shī'a exegeses in chronological order. It
looks at the most important Shī'a exegeses produced throughout
the history of this discipline (Suyūṭī, 1363 AHS/1983, vol. 4, pp.
233-244; Ṭāshkūprīzāda, vol. 1, pp. 439-500; *'Ulūm al-Qur'an 'ind
al-Mufassirīn*, vol. 3, pp. 423-483).

3. The third category consists of the works that analyse the
various exegetic methodologies. Such works, which are of a
relatively recent authorship, may be found in three forms.

One form comprises those works that are exhaustive in scope,
including every methodology and persuasion. The earliest such
work is that written by Hungarian orientalist, Ignaz Goldziher
(d. 1921), which has been translated into Arabic under the title
Madhāhib al-Tafsīr al-Islāmī (Egypt: 1374/1954; for further details,
see section 14, Orientalists and Qur'anic Exegesis).

This line of work was followed up in *al-Tafsīr wa al-Mufassirūn* by Muḥammad Ḥusayn Dhahabī, professor of Qur'anic sciences at the Al-Azhar University in Cairo. This two-volume text, considered as the most authoritative in this field, contains three sections. Sections one and two examine the development of Qur'anic exegesis during the period of the Companions and the Successors. Section three, which forms the bulk of the book, surveys the various exegetic tendencies and methodologies from all theological and jurisprudential schools that developed subsequent to the ʿAbbāsid Dynasty, thereafter going into further detail as to the most prominent exegets and exegeses throughout the entire history of the discipline while shedding light on their methodologies. The book's introduction offers some general points concerning interpretation and translation, and the author ends the book with an exposition and analysis of the recent trends in Qur'anic exegesis. Dhahabī, who wrote his book in 1946, claims to have broken new ground in his comprehensive treatment of this topic (Dhahabī, vol. 1, pp. 8-9). Dhahabī's major flaw in this work is his biased attacks. His critique of Shīʿa works is so charged with sectarian prejudice that he proclaims them as being of no value (Ayāzī, p. 21; Maʿrifat, vol. 1, publisher's foreword, p. 4). His unpublished writings in which he denounced and derided the Shīʿa school were gathered and published posthumously by Muḥammad Anwar Bultājī as the third volume of his work (Dhahabī, vol. 3, Bultājī's introduction, p. 3).

Contemporary scholar of Qur'anic studies, Muḥammad Hādī Maʿrifat, wrote his *al-Tafsīr wa al-Mufassirūn fī Thawba al-Qashīb* in two volumes in the same vein. The overall form and outlines of this book resemble Dhahabī's work. In the course of the first volume, Maʿrifat offers an extensive examination of such topics as relate to Qur'anic exegesis, Qur'anic translation, the development of Qur'anic exegesis during the Prophet's lifetime and its progress during the period of the Companions and the Successors, and finally the role of the Prophet's Household in the advancement of this discipline. The author devotes the second volume to the final stage in the development of Qur'anic exegesis: the authorship of Qur'anic exegeses. He distinguishes two principal methods in Qur'anic exegesis, interpretation by recourse to transmitted material (*tafsīr bi-'l-ma'thūr*) and interpretation based on independent judgment (*tafsīr ijtihādī*), and he then goes on to divide each of these two into narrower approaches, studying the most renowned figures of each approach and examining a majority of the prominent exegeses.

Manāhij al-Mufassirīn (Beirut: 1980), coauthored by Musā'id Muslim Āl Ja'far and Muḥyī Hilāl Sarḥān, is another work belonging to this category. The first part of the work examines the conception and development of Qur'anic exegesis; in the second part, interpretation by recourse to transmitted material and independent judgment are the focus; and in the third part, lexical, grammatical, jurisprudential, and theological approaches to Qur'anic exegesis are dealt with, and the book ends by introducing a new approach. When considering a method or approach, the authors assess and analyse the exegeses pertaining thereto.

Manī' 'Abd al-Ḥalīm Maḥmūd has also authored a work entitled *Manāhij al-Mufassirīn* (Beirut: 1978) but with a different approach. In lieu of studying the various exegetic methods and arranging his book in accordance to those methods, he treats of fifty two exegets along with their exegeses in chronological order.

The second form comprises studies that confine their scope to a single era or to a single method or approach. Some of these discuss and evaluate the transmitted method alone, such as *al-Manhaj al-Atharī fī Tafsīr al-Qur'an al-Karīm* (Qum: 1372 AHS/1993-1994) by Hudā Jāsim Muḥammad Abū Ṭabra and *al-Tafsīr bi-'l-Ma'thūr wa Taṭawwuruh 'inda al-Shī'a al-Imāmiyya* (Beirut: 2000) by Iḥsān Amīn. Traditions of biblical origin (*Isrā'īliyyāt*) and forged reports constitute one of the topics related to transmitted exegesis, and *al-Isrā'īliyyāt wa al-Mawḍū'āt fī Kutub al-Tafsīr* (Damascus: 1390/1970-1971) by Muḥammad Muḥammad Abū Shuhba addresses this topic.

Some works, on the other hand, take up the interpretation based on independent judgment and discretion as their topic. One such work is *al-Tafsīr bi-'l-Ra'y: Qawā'iduh wa Ḍawābiṭuh wa A'lāmuh* (Damascus: 1999) by Muḥammad Ḥamd Zaghlūl.

Some of these works choose a certain period out of the long history of this discipline, investigating the peculiar tendencies of the exegeses of the period in question. *Tafsīr al-Ṣaḥāba: Mumayyizātuh, Khaṣā'iṣuh, Maṣādiruh, Qīmatuh al-'Ilmiyya* (Cairo: n.d.) by Muḥammad 'Abd al-Raḥīm; *Tafsīr al-Tābi'īn: 'Arḍ wa Dirāsa Muqārana* (Riyadh: 1999) by Muḥammd ibn 'Abd Allāh ibn 'Alī Khuḍayrī; and *Athar al-Taṭawwur al-Fikrī fī al-Tafsīr fī al-'Aṣr al-'Abbāsī* (Beirut: 1984) by Muslim 'Abd Allāh Āl Ja'far are three such works. And as Qur'anic exegesis took on a new form in the fourteenth/twentieth century, which may be designated as a new method of Qur'anic exegesis, certain works have been produced to assess this new trend. A number of these works are as follows: *Ittijāhāt al-Tafsīr fī al-'Aṣr al-Rāhin* (Amman: 1402/1982) by 'Abd al-Majīd 'Abd al-Salām Muḥtasib; *Ittijāhāt al-Tafsīr fī al-Qarn al-Rābi' 'Ashar* (Riyadh: 1407/1987) by Fahd ibn 'Abd al-Raḥmān ibn Sulaymān Rūmī; *'Aqlgarā'ī dar Tafāsīr-i Qarn-i Chahārdahum* (Qum: 1379 AHS/2000) by Shādī Nafīsī. Occasionally the topic of study may be restricted to the exegeses produced in a certain region, such as *Madrasa al-Tafsīr fī al-Andalus* (Beirut: 1404/1984) by Muṣṭafā Ibrāhīm Mushaynī.

Some works are mainly concerned with the examination and analysis of one of the predominant exegetic methods. The following books take this approach: *al-Tafsīr al-'Ilmī li-'l-Qur'an fī al-Mīzān* (Beirut: 1991) by Aḥmad 'Umar Abū Ḥujr; *Tafsīr-i Kalāmī-yi Qur'an-i Majīd* (Tehran: 1370 AHS/1991) by Muḥammad Ḥusayn Rawḥānī; *al-Tafsīr al-Mawḍ'ī bayn al-Naẓariyya wa al-Taṭbīq* (Amman: 1997) by Ṣalāḥ 'Abd al-Fattāḥ Khālidī; *al-Manhaj al-Balāghī li-Tafsīr al-Qur'an al-Karīm* (Beirut: 1997) by Ḥasan Mas'ūd Ṭuwayr; *al-Tafsīr al-Lughawī li-al-Qur'an al-Karīm* (Riyadh: 1422/2001-2002) by Musā'id ibn Sulaymān ibn Nāṣir Ṭayyār; *al-Manhaj al-Bayānī fī Tafsīr al-Qur'an al-

Karīm (Maktaba al-Injil al-Miṣriyya: 1981) by Kāmil 'Alī Sa'fān.

The third form in which these studies appear consists of those that analyse and evaluate a single work and the approach taken by its author. Numerous books have been produced to date evaluating the exegeses of various periods within the Sunnī school, from the early stages of this discipline to the contemporary period, shedding light on the methodology espoused by their authors. A list of works that fall into this category is as follows: (1) *Mujāhid: al-Mufassir wa al-Tafsīr* (Cairo: 1411/1991) by Aḥmad Ismā'īl Nawfal; (2) *Ibn Jarīr wa Manhajuh fī al-Tafsīr* (Cairo: 1411/1991) by Muḥammad Bakr Ismā'īl; (3) *al-Baghawī wa Manhajuh fī al-Tafsīr* (Amman: 1402/1982) by 'Affāf 'Abd al-Ghafūr; (4) *al-Zamakhsharī Lughawiyyan wa Mufassiran* (Cairo: 1977) by Murtaḍā Āyatullāhzāda Shīrāzī; (5) *al-Rāzī Mufassiran* (Baghdad: 1394/1974) by Muḥsin 'Abd al-Ḥamīd; (6) *al-Qāḍī al-Bayḍāwī al-Mufassir* (Damascus: 1407/1987) by Muḥammad Zuḥaylī; (7) *Ibn Taymiyya wa Juhūduh fī al-Tafsīr* (Beirut: 1405/1984) by Ibrāhīm Khalīl Baraka; (8) *al-'Ajīb wa al-Gharīb fī Tafsīr al-Qur'an: Tafsīr Ibn Kathīr Numūdhajan* (Tunisia: 2001) by Waḥīd Sa'fī; (9) *al-Ālūsī Mufassiran* (Baghdad: 1388/1968) by Muḥsin 'Abd al-Ḥamīd; (10) *al-Qāsimī wa Manhajuh fī al-Tafsīr* (Cairo: 1411/1991) by Muḥammad Bakr Ismā'īl; (11) *Manhaj al-Imām 'Abduh fī Tafsīr al-Qur'an al-Karīm* (Cairo: n.d.) by 'Abd Allāh Maḥmūd Shaḥḥāta; (12) *Fī Ẓilāl al-Qur'an fī al-Mīzān* (Jiddah: 1406/1986) by Ṣalāḥ 'Abd al-Fattāḥ Khālidī; (13) *Muḥammad 'Izza Darwaza wa Tafsīr al-Qur'an al-Karīm* (Riyadh: 1414/1994) by Farīd Muṣṭafā Sulaymān.

There are works in this vein dealing with Shī'a exegetes. The following are some examples: (1) *al-Shaykh al-Ṭūsī Mufassiran* (Qum: 1378 AHS/1999) by Muḥammad Ḥusayn Āl Yāsīn; (2) *Ṭabarsī wa Majma' al-Bayān* (Tehran: 1361 AHS/1982) by Ḥusayn Karīmān; (3) *al-Ṭabāṭabā'ī wa Manhajuh fī Tafsīr al-Qur'an* (Tehran: 1405/1985) by 'Alī Awsī. (It is to be noted that there are many other works on this topic that are in the form of academic theses and as such have not been published. To learn more regarding works concerning exegetic methodologies and the specifications of the theses in this relation, see *Dānishnāma-yi Qur'an wa Qur'an-pazhūhī*, vol. 2, pp. 1806-1820; Āshūrī, ibid; Ayāzī, the section entitled *Dirāsāt Ḥawl al-Tafsīr* following the presentation of each exegetic work.)

14. ORIENTALIST AND QUR'ANIC EXEGESIS

Muḥhamad Kāẓim Raḥmatī

One may distinguish three stages in the orientalists' studies of Qur'anic interpretation determined in the main by their attitude toward Islamic studies in general. The first stage may be dated from around the end of the first/seventh century. John of Damascus (fl. c. 132-135/676-754) may be pointed out as the most prominent figure of this stage. He wrote a treatise denouncing Islam, which contained criticisms of the Qur'an (Sahas, pp. 74-93). Apparently, he was acquainted with Arabic and thus studied the Qur'an in its original language (Versteech, p. 54; cf. Sahas, p. 46).

For the next several centuries, the only source on the Qur'an available to the Westerners consisted of such denunciatory apologetics written by Christian theologians against Islam, which drew mainly on secondhand sources and previously written apologetic works against Islam (Versteech, p. 55; for a list of the works written in this vein, see Daniel, pp. 414-438; Bobzin, pp. 195, 202-204). The complete translation of the Qur'an into Latin, commissioned by Peter the Venerable (1092-1156), which appeared in around 1143 CE constituted a watershed in this trend (Versteech, p. 55; Bobzin, p. 194; Daniel, p. 22; Fück, pp. 15-19). This translation, which was published along with anti-Islamic apologetic works by Peter the Venerable and Petrus Alphonsi (d. 1110), was the first comprehensive work on Islam and the Qur'an and played an important role in shaping the European mindset vis-à-vis Islam (Rezvan, p. 42; see also Translation of the Qur'an, section 3: into other languages).

The publication of Nöldeke's *History of the Qur'an* (*Geschichte des Korans*) in 1859 ushered in a new stage of Qur'anic studies. Due to its comprehensiveness in considering a wide range of Qur'anic topics, this work succeeded in drawing Western intellectuals to the study of the Qur'an. The tradition of Qur'anic studies that developed in Germany was characterised by a prevailing lexical interest and was influenced by the tradition of biblical scholarship. Gustav Flügel (1802-1870) published the Qur'an for the first time in Europe in 1834, offering an index of the Qur'an in 1842 entitled *Concordantiae Corani arabicae* (Rezvan, p. 46).

The orientalists who studied the Qur'an after Nöldeke—such as Otto Pretzl (1893-1941) and Gotthelf Bergsträsser (1886-1933;)—were mainly his students and were therefore strongly influenced by his work.

Rudi Paret (1901-1983) and Régis Blachère (1900-1073) are two other orientalists who took up the study of Arabic philology and a linguistic analysis of the Qur'an. In his translation of the Qur'an, Rudi Paret pursues a comparative analysis of words based on their usage and application in Arabic literature. He provides a detailed account of his studies in his *Der Koran, Kommentar und Konkordanz*. Blachère in his studies makes use of pre-Islamic Arabic poetry and literature (Rezvan, p. 47).

For names of other Qur'anologists of this period one may mention, among others, Arthur Jeffery (1892-1959), Richard Bell (1876-1952), Alphonse Mingana, and Charles Cutler Torrey. For

Qur'anologists of this period an important topic was to shed light on the Qur'an's sources in its recounting the stories of the Old and New Testaments and other sacred scriptures (Bargnīsī, p. 99). The central question that occupied them was to what extent the Qur'an drew on Judaic and Christian sources. This topic was first broached by Abraham Geiger in his book entitled *Was hat Mohammed aus dem Judentume aufgenommen* (Rezvan, p. 46, fn. 40).

The most prolific orientalist of this period was Arthur Jeffery. He edited *Muqaddima al-Muḥarrar al-Wajīz* by Ibn ʿAṭiyya Andalusī (d. 546/1152) and *al-Mabānī fī Naẓm al-Maʿānī*, publishing these two treatises in one volume under the title *Muqaddimatān fī ʿUlūm al-Qur'an* (Cairo: 1ˢᵗ ed. 1954, 2ⁿᵈ ed. 1972). He also wrote two essays concerning *al-Hidāya wa al-ʿIrfān fī Tafsīr al-Qur'an bi-'l-Qur'an* (a work by Muḥammad Abū Zayd, contemporary Qur'anic exegete, which was banned from publication in Egypt; Karīmīnīyā, p. 401; to read more about this Qur'anic exegesis, see Dhahabī, vol. 2, pp. 584-600).

As of 1950, Qur'anic studies underwent certain transformations in the approach to exegetic concerns. The changes brought about by modernist trends in Qur'anic exegesis, especially in Egypt, attracted the attention of many orientalists. Western Qur'anologists focused increasingly greater attention on the new scientific and literary trends in Qur'anic exegesis emerging in Egypt. One of the most prominent scholars to write on these new trends was Jacques Jomier. He wrote extensively on a range of topics and exegeses, such as Muḥammad Rashīd Riḍā's (d. 1935) *Tafsīr al-Manār* based on notes he had collected from the lectures by his teacher, Muḥammad ʿAbduh (d. 1905), the opinions of Amīn Khūlī, the founder of the literary approach to Qur'anic exegesis in Egypt, Ṭanṭāwī's *al-Jawāhir fī Tafsīr al-Qur'an*, a leading example of scientific exegesis, and the emergence of the new exegetic movement in Egypt during the years 1947-1951 (Rippin, pp. 236-237).

The most prominent work on Qur'anic exegesis produced after Nöldeke's *History of the Qur'an* is Ignaz Goldziher's *Die*

Richtungen Der Islamischen Koranauslegung. Johannes Marinus Simon Baljon, in completing the last chapter of Goldziher's afore-mentioned work, examined the exegetic trend in Egypt in the years 1880-1960. In his studies, Baljon considered such exegetes as Khalaf Allāh and Muḥammad Kāmil Ḥusayn and also Urdu-speaking Qur'anic exegets such as Abū al-Kalām Āzād. Another Western scholar to treat of the modern trend of Qur'anic exegesis in Egypt is Johannes Jansen, whose book on this topic is entitled *The Interpretation of the Koran in Modern Egypt.*

Writing monographs on specific exegets is another approach orientalists take in studying Qur'anic exegesis. In this genre, topics of interest are the exegets, their methodologies, and their peculiar views. Scholars who have written in this genre are, among others, Marc Chartier, Freeland Abbott, Issa Boullata, Yvonne Yazbeck Haddad, and de Jong. Marc Chartier has produced articles concerning the exegets Muṣṭafā Maḥmūd (*Mujādala li-Fahm 'Aṣrī li-'l-Qur'an*) and Muḥammad Aḥmad Khalaf Allāh (Anīs, p. 60). Freeland Abbott and Charles Adams have examined Abū al-A'lā Mawdūdī's *Tafhīm al-Qur'an*; Issa Boullata has written on the literary interpretation, especially in reference to the opinions of 'Ā'isha 'Abd al-Raḥmān bint al-Shāṭī (*al-Tafsīr al-Bayānī li-al-Qur'an al-Karīm*); Yāzbak Ḥaddād has focused on Sayyid Quṭb's *Fī Ẓilāl al-Qur'an*; and de Jong has given special attention to Ṭanṭāwī's *Jawāhir* (Rippin, p. 237).

Another genre that has emerged in recent years in studying Qur'anic exegesis is what may be termed "verse analysis." There are two approaches within this genre: one is juridico-theological analysis, and the other is historical analysis. In this genre, the verses are scrutinised for their juridical, theological, or historical significance. The general purpose pursued in this genre is to reconstruct the historical context within which Muslim exegetes understood the Qur'an. The articles produced by John Burton and G. R. Hawting are examples of studies of verses in view of their juridical and theological significance. Uri Rubin has authored articles concerning the historical background of

Qur'anic verses (Karīmīniyā, pp. 422-423). A number of articles by Andrew Rippin have been collected into one book, published under the title *The Qur'an and Its Interpretative Tradition*. Surveying early exegetic texts such as *Jāmi' al-Bayān 'an Ta'wīl Āyī al-Qur'an* and the exegeses by Hūd ibn Muḥakkam Huwwārī Ibāḍī and Muqātil ibn Sulaymān have been the focus of Claude Gilliot's studies on Qur'anic exegesis (Index Islamicus, 1997, p. 36; Karīmīniyā, pp. 392-394).

In studying the early exegetic works, orientalists take two different approaches. One approach consists in scrutinising the reports contained in the exegetic texts. This approach hinges largely on the analysis of the various reports recorded in religious biographies and comparing the myriad chains of transmission of the reports in the exegetic corpus. This approach is taken up in the articles by Isiah Goldfeld in which he examines the exegeses by Ibn 'Abbās and Muqātil ibn Sulaymān, in the studies carried out by Fred Leemhuis on Mujāhid ibn Jabr, and in Ḥamad Ṣammūd's work on Yaḥyā ibn Salām (d. 200/815-816; Rippin, pp. 229-230).

Literary analysis of exegetic texts constitutes the second approach. This approach developed largely as the result of Goldziher's attempts on proving the spuriousness of many a report in the religious and especially the exegetic corpus. He employed certain literary criteria in order to determine the historical period in which these reports were fabricated. Nevertheless, the founder of this approach was John Wansbrough, who was convinced that in its development Qur'anic exegesis underwent five main phases—(1) exegesis based on transmitted reports (*riwāyāt*; 2) juridical exegesis, (3) textual exegesis, (4) rhetorical (or literary) exegesis, and (5) analogical exegesis—the distinctive characteristics of which he details (pp. 119-227; see also *Encyclopedia of Religion*, "*Tafsīr*").

Examination of the exegetic corpus with a view to theological themes forms the topic of a number of scholarly works in this field. For examples of works in this vein, we may point to the articles by Manfred Götz (concerning mainly Abū Manṣūr Māturīdī's *Ta'wīlāt al-Qur'an*) and the book by Meir Mikhael Bar-Asher on early Shī'a exegesis.

Gerhard Böwering, Michelle Alard, Paul Noya, Gramlisch, and Grille consider mystical exegesis of the Qur'an.

Menachem Krister, Khoury, Gerard Le Comte, and Gordon Newby study Qur'anic exegeses in view of their treatment of the stories of the prophets and other such elements that resemble Biblical literature (Rippin, p. 234). An important work that takes this topic as its subject is Haim Schwarzbaum's *Biblical and Extra-Biblical Legends in Islamic Folk-Literature*. Despite its lack of substance, this book has gained special prominence due to its extensive and comprehensive bibliography, which provides an exhaustive list of the sources in this field (ibid.). Another important work in this genre is *The Historical Dictionary of Prophets in Islam and Judaism* coauthored by Brannon Wheeler and Scott Noegel, which also contains an impressive bibliography. In *Prophets in the Quran: An Introduction to the Quran and Muslim Exegesis*, Wheeler provides a comparative study between the opinions of Muslim exegetes and Biblical literature. Wheeler's most important work, however, is *Moses in the Qur'an and Islamic Exegesis*, which is published by Curzon Press.

Reconstructing Qur'anic exegeses that are no longer extant is yet another field of interest to orientalists. Daniel Jimaret's extensive research on the Qur'anic exegesis by Abū 'Alī Jubbā'ī is one such effort into reconstructing a lost Qur'anic exegesis. But on the other hand, orientalists have generally shown to be uninterested in editing and republishing old Qur'anic exegeses. The only notable attempts at editing old manuscripts of Qur'anic exegeses are the publication of the introductions to *al-Mabānī* and to *al-Muḥarrar al-Wajīz* (edited by Arthur Jeffery), the introduction to Tha'labī's *al-Kashf wa al-Bayān*, and Muqātil ibn Sulaymān's *Khahms Mi'a Āya min al-Qur'an* (the latter two edited by Goldfeld).

Goldziher's *Die Richtungen Der Islamischen Koranauslegung*

has remained a respected reference book for scholars in this field due to its comprehensive study of the development of the science of Qur'anic exegesis and the various methodologies involved therein. Nevertheless, this book has certain shortcomings, which has led scholars to write articles and essays to complement it (Rippin's introduction to *Approaches to the History of the Interpretation of the Qur'an*). The need for an updated source to replace Goldziher's work occasioned a conference at the University of Calgary in 1985. The articles contributed at that conference were collected and published under the title *Approaches to the History of the Interpretation of the Qur'an*. In this relation, one may also point to the twenty fifth volume (entitled *The Qur'an: Formative Interpretation*, edited by Andrew Rippin) of the forty-seven-volume *The Formation of the Classical Islamic World*, which contains a number of important articles on Qur'anic exegesis authored by orientalists.

Adel Theodore Khoury, Catholic priest and theologian, who before his retirement was a professor at the theology department of the University of Münster, Germany, has translated the Qur'an, along with some exposition, into German, which has been published in twelve volumes. His method in this work is to offer the original Arabic of a verse, then its translation, and finally its exposition. He is especially interested in morphology and syntax, considering also the occasions of revelation of Qur'anic verses. In creating this voluminous work, the author has made use of the works of many authoritative Qur'anic exegetes, such as Bayḍāwī, Ibn Kathīr, Fakhr Rāzī, Shaykh Ṭūsī, and ʿAllāma Ṭabāṭabā'ī.

A number of books have also been written that list the exegetic studies and research conducted by orientalists. In this relation, one may cite Murtiḍā Karīmīnīyā's *Kitāb-shināsī-yi Muṭāliʿāt-i Qur'anī bi-Zabān-hā-yi Urūpā'ī* (Tehran: 1380 AHS/2002), books and articles by Munawwar Aḥmad Anīs and Andrew Rippin, and Najīb ʿAqīqī's brief report (vol. 3, pp. 531-541).

BIBLIOGRAPHY

'Abd Allah ibn Aḥmad Nasafī, *Tafsīr al-Qur'an al-Jalīl al-Musammā bi-Madārik al-Tanzīl wa Ḥaqā'iq al-Ta'wīl*, Dār al-Kitāb al-'Arabī, Beirut [n.d.].

'Abd Allah ibn Ḥusayn 'Ukbarī, *al-Tibyān fī I'rāb al-Qur'an*, 'Alī Muḥammad Bajāwī, [Cairo 1976], Beirut offset reprint 1407/1987.

'Abd Allah ibn Ḥusayn 'Ukbarī, *Imlā' mā Manna bi-hi al-Raḥmān min Wujūh al-I'rāb wa al-Qirā'āt fī Jamī' al-Qur'an*, Ibrāhīm 'Aṭwa 'Awaḍ, ed., Cairo 1389/1969, Tehran offset reprint 1361 AHS/1982.

'Abd Allah ibn Muḥammad Najm Rāzī, *Mirṣād al-'Ibād*, Muḥammad Amīn Riyāḥī, ed., Tehran 1361 AHS/1982.

'Abd Allah ibn Sulaymān Sijistānī, *Kitāb al-Maṣāḥif*, Beirut 1405/1985.

'Abd Allah ibn 'Umar Bayḍāwī, *Anwār al-Tanzī wa Asrār al-Ta'wīl*, Egypt 1388/1968, Tehran offset reprint 1363 AHS/1984.

'Abd Allah Maḥmūd Shaḥḥāta, *Ta'rīkh al-Qur'an wa al-Tafsīr*, Egypt 1392/1972.

'Abd 'Alī ibn Jum'a Ḥuwayzī, *Tafsīr Nūr al-Thiqalayn*, Hāshim Rasūlī Maḥallātī, Qum 1412/1991.

'Abd al-'Azīz Sayyid Ahl, *Min Ishārāt al-'Ulūm fī al-Qur'an al-Karīm*, Beirut [1392/1972?].

'Abd al-Ghaffār 'Abd al-Raḥīm, *al-Imām Muḥmmad 'Abduh wa Manhajuhu fī al-Tafsīr*, [Cairo 1400/1980?].

'Abd al-Ḥusayn Zarrīnkūb, *Sirr-i Niy: Naqd wa Sharḥ-i Taḥlīlī wa Taṭbīqī-yi Mathnawī*, Tehran 1364 AHS/1985.

'Abd al-Karīm ibn Hawāzin Qushayrī, *Laṭā'if al-Ishārāt*, Ibrāhīm Basyūnī, ed., Cairo 1981-1983.

'Abd al-Karīm Surūsh, "Ta'wīl dar Mathnawī," in: *Nāmih-yi Shahīdī: Jashn-nāmih-yi Ustād Duktur Sayyid Ja'far Shahīdī*, 'Alī Asghar Muḥammadkhānī, ed., Ṭarḥ-i Nuw, Tehran 1374 AHS/1995.

'Abd al-Majīd 'Abd al-Salām Muḥtasib, *Ittijāhāt al-Tafsīr fī al-'Aṣr al-Rāhin*, Amman 1402/1982.

'Abd al-Mun'im Nimr, *'Ilm al-Tafsīr: Kayf Nash'a wa Taṭawwur ḥatā Intahā ilā 'Aṣrinā al-Ḥāḍir*, Cairo 1405/1985.

'Abd al-Qāhir ibn 'Abd al-Raḥmān Jurjānī, *Dalā'il al-I'jāz*, Muḥammad Rashīd Riḍā, ed., Beirut 1398/1978.

'Abd al-Raḥmān 'Akk, *Uṣūl al-Tafsīr wa Qawā'iduhū*, Beirut 1407/1986.

'Abd al-Raḥmān ibn Abī Bakr Suyūṭī, *Bughiyat al-Wu'āt fī Ṭabaqāt al-Lughawiyyīn wa al-Nuḥāt*, Muḥammad Abū al-Faḍl Ibrāhīm, ed., Cairo 1384/1964.

'Abd al-Raḥmān ibn Abī Bakr Suyūṭī, *al-Durr al-Manthūr fī al-Tafsīr bi-'l-Ma'thūr*, Qum 1404/1983.

'Abd al-Raḥmān ibn Abī Bakr Suyūṭī, *al-Itqān fī 'Ulūm al-Qur'an*, Muḥammad Abū al-Faḍl Ibrāhīm, ed., Cairo 1967, Qum offset reprint 1363 AHS/1984.

'Abd al-Raḥmān ibn Abī Bakr al-Suyūṭī, *Kitāb Ṭabaqāt al-Mufassirīn*, Meursinge, Leiden 1839, Tehran offset edition 1960.

'Abd al-Raḥmān ibn Abī Bakr Suyūṭī, *al-Taḥbīr fī 'Ilm al-Tafsīr*, Beirut 1408/1988.

'Abd al-Raḥmān ibn Muḥammad Tha'ālibī, *al-Jawāhir al-Ḥisān fī Tafsīr al-Qur'an*, Abū Muḥammad Ghumārī Idrīsī Ḥasanī, Beirut 1416/1996.

'Abd al-Raḥmān ibn Muḥammad Tha'ālibī, *al-Jawāhir al-Ḥisān fī Tafsīr al-Qur'an*, 'Abd al-Fattāḥ Abū Sinna, 'Alī Muḥammad Mu'awwaḍ, 'Ādil Aḥmad 'Abd al-Mawjūd, eds., Beirut 1418/1997.

'Abd al-Salām Aḥmad Ganūnī, *al-Madrasa al-Qur'aniyya fī al-Maghrib min al-Fatḥ al-Islāmī ila Ibn 'Aṭiyya*, vol. 1, Rabat 1401/1981.

'Abd al-Wahhāb ibn Aḥmad Sha'rānī, *Ṭabaqāt al-Kubrā*, Beirut 1408/1988.

Abū 'Alī Fārsī, *al-Ḥujja li-'l-Qurrā' al-Sab'a*, Badr al-Dīn Qahwajī, Bashīr Juwayjātī, eds., Damascus 1404/1984.

Abū al-Futūḥ Rāzī, *Tafsīr Rawḍ al-Jinān wa Rawḥ al-Janān fī Tafsīr al-Qur'an*, Muḥammad Ja'far Yāḥaqī, Muḥammad Mahdī Nāṣiḥ, eds., Mashhad 1365-1376 AHS/1986-1997.

Abū Ḥayyān Gharnāṭī, *Tafsīr al-Baḥr al-Muḥīṭ*, Beirut 1403/1983.

Abū Ḥayyān Gharnāṭī, *Tuḥfa al-Arīb bi-mā fī al-Qur'an min al-Gharīb*, Aḥmad Maṭlūb, Khadīja Ḥadīthī, eds., Baghdad 1379/1977.

Abū Ja'far Muḥammad ibn Jarīr al-Ṭabarī, *Jāmi' al-Bayān Ta'wīl Āy al-Qur'an*, Ṣidqī Majīl al-'Aṭṭār, ed., introduction by Khalīl al-Mays, Dār al-Fikr, Beirut 1426/2005.

Abū Naṣr Sarrāj, *Kitāb al-Luma' fī al-Taṣawwuf*, Reynold Allen Nicholson, ed., Leyden 1914, Tehran offset reprint [n.d.].

Abū Ṭālib Makkī, *Kitāb Qūt al-Qulūb fī Mu'āmila al-Maḥbūb wa Waṣf Ṭarīq al-Murīd ila Maqām al-Tawḥīd*, Cairo 1310/1892, Beirut offset reprint [n.d.].

Abū al-Yaqdān 'Aṭiyya Jubūrī, *Dirāsāt fī Tafsīr wa Rijālihi*, Cairo [1971].

Adam Metz, *Tamaddun-i Islāmī dar Qarn-i Chahārum yā Runisāns-i Islāmī*, 'Alīriḍā Dhakāvatī Qarāguzlū, tr., Tehran 1364 AHS/1985.

Aḥmad 'Alī Bābā'ī, Riḍā Muḥammadī, *Fihrist-i Mawḍū'ī-yi Tafsīr-i Nimūnih*, Qum 1376 AHS/1997.

Aḥmad ibn 'Abd Allah Abū Nu'aym, *Ḥilyat al-Awliyā' wa Ṭabaqāt al-Aṣfiyā'*, Beirut 1387/1967.

Aḥmad ibn 'Alī Nasā'ī, *Kitāb al-Sunan al-Kubrā*, 'Abd al-Ghaffār Sulaymān Bundārī, Kasrawī Ḥasan, eds., Beirut 1411/1991.

Aḥmad ibn Muḥammad Abū 'Ubayd Hirawī, *Kitāb al-Gharībayn: Gharībay al-Qur'an wa al-Ḥadīth*, Ḥaydarābād Dakkan 1406-1407/1985-1986.

Aḥmad ibn Muḥammad Fayyūmī, *al-Miṣbāḥ al-Munīr*, Beirut 1987.

Aḥmad ibn Muḥammad Ghazālī, *Sawāniḥ*, Naṣr Allah Pūrjavādī, ed., Tehran 1359 AHS/1981.

Aḥmad ibn Muḥammad Ḥaddādī Samarqandī, *al-Madkhal li-'Ilm Tafsīr Kitāb Allah Ta'ālā*, Ṣafwān 'Adnān Dāwūdī, ed., Damascus 1408/1988.

Aḥmad ibn Muḥammad Maybudī, *Kashf al-Asrār wa 'Uddat al-Abrār*, 'Alī Asghar Ḥikmat, ed., Tehran 1361 AHS/1982.

Aḥmad ibn Muṣṭafā Ṭāshkuprīzādih, *Miftāḥ al-Sa'āda wa Miṣbāḥ al-Siyāda*, vol. 2, Ḥaydarābād Dakkan 1400/1980.

Aḥmad ibn Yaḥyā Balādhurī, *Ansāb al-Ashrāf*, Muḥammad Bāqir Maḥmūdī, ed., Beirut 1394/1974.

Aḥmad Muḥammad Ḥawfī, *al-Zamakhsharī*, al-Hay'a al-Miṣriyya al-'Āmma li-'l-Kitāb, Egypt [n.d.].

Aḥmad 'Umar Abū Ḥijr, *Tafsīr al-'Ilmī li-'al-Qur'an fī al-Mīzān*, Beirut 1411/1991.

Akbar Hāshimī Rafsanjānī, *Tafsīr-i Rāhnamā: Ravishī Nu dar Irā'ih-yi Mafāhīm va Muḍū'āt-i Qur'an*, Qum 1371 AHS/1992-

'Alī Akbar Bābā'ī, Ghulām'alī 'Azīzī Kiyā, Mujtabā Rūḥānīrād, *Rawish-shināsī-yi Tafsīr-i Qur'an*, Qum 1379 AHS/2000..

'Alī ibn Abī Ṭālib, *Nahj al-Balāgha*, Ṣubḥī Ṣāliḥ, ed., Beirut [1387/1967?], Qum offset reprint [n.d.].

'Alī ibn Ḥusām al-Dīn Mutaqqī, *Kanz al-'Ummāl fī Sunan al-Aqwāl wa al-Af'āl*, Bakrī Ḥayyānī, Ṣafwa Saqqā, eds., Beirut 1409/1989.

'Alī ibn Ḥusayn 'Alam al-Hudā, *Amālī al-Murtaḍā: Ghurar al-Fawā'id wa Durar al-Qalā'id*, Muḥammad Abū al-Faḍl Ibrāhīm, ed., Cairo 1373/1954, Tehran offset reprint [n.d.].

'Alī ibn Muḥammad Jurjānī, *Kitāb al-Ta'rīfāt*, Ibrāhīm Muḥammad Abyārī, ed., Beirut 1405/1985.

'Alī ibn Muḥammad Khāzin, *Lubāb al-Ta'wīl fī Ma'ānī al-Tanzīl*, in: *Majma' al-Tafāsīr*, [Cairo] 1317-1320/1899-1902, Istanbul offset reprint, Dār al-Da'wa 1404/1984.

'Alī ibn 'Uthmān Hujwīrī, *Kashf al-Mahjūb*, V. Zhukovsky, ed., Leningrad 1926, Tehran offset reprint 1358 AHS/1980.

'Alīnaqī Munzavī, *Fihrist-i Kitābkhānih-yi Ihdā'ī-yi Āqā-yi Sayyid Muḥammad Mishkāt bih Kitābkhānih-yi Danishgāh-i Tihrān*, vols. 1-2, Tehran 1330-1332 AHS/1951-1953.

Amīn Khūlī, *al-A'māl al-Kāmila*, vol. 10: *Manāhij Tajdīd fī al-Naḥw wa al-Balāgha wa al-Tafsīr wa Adab*, [Cairo] 1995.

Amīn Khūlī, "al-Tafsīr, Takmila," *Dā'irat al-Ma'ārif al-Islāmiyya*, Dār al-Sha'b, Cairo [1969?].

'Amr ibn Baḥr Jāḥiẓ, *Kitāb al-Ḥayawān*, 'Abd al-Salām Muḥammad Hārūn, ed., Egypt [1385-1389/1965-1969 ?], Beirut offset reprint 1388/1969.

'Amr ibn 'Uthmān Sībawayh, 'Abd al-Salam Muḥammad Hārūn, ed., Cairo [1385/1966], Beirut offset reprint 1411/1991.

Bahā' al-Dīn Khurramshāhī, *Tafsīr va Tafāsīr-i Jadīd*, Tehran 1364 AHS/1985.

Dāryūsh Shāygān, Henri Corbin, *Āfāq-i Tafakkur-i Ma'navī dar Islām-i Īrānī*, Baqir Parhām, tr., Tehran, 1371 AHS/1992.

Faḍl ibn Ḥasan Ṭabarsī, *Majma' al-Bayān fī Tafsīr al-Qur'an*, Hāshim Rasūlī Maḥallātī, Faḍl Allah Yazdī Ṭabāṭabā'ī, eds., Beirut 1408/1988.

Faḍl ibn Ḥasan Ṭabarsī, *Tafsīr Jawāmi' al-Jāmi'*, vol. 1, Abū al-Qāsim Gurjī, ed., Tehran 1347 AHS/1968.

Fahd ibn 'Abd al-Raḥmān Rūmī, *Buḥūth fī Uṣūl al-Tafsīr wa Manāhijihī*, Riyadh 1419/1998.

Fahd ibn 'Abd al-Raḥmān Rūmī, *Ittijāhāt al-Tafsīr fī al-Qarn al-Rābi' 'Ashar*, Riyadh 1407/1986.

Fakhr al-Dīn ibn Muḥammad Ṭurayḥī, *Majma' al-Baḥrayn*, Aḥmad Ḥusaynī, ed., Tehran 1362 AHS/1983.

Fu'ād Sizgīn, *Ta'rīkh al-Turāth al-'Arabī*, vol. 1, pt. 1, translated into Arabic by Maḥmūd Fahmī Ḥijāzī, Riyadh 1403/1983.

Ḥamīd 'Ināyat, "Tajaddud-i Fikr-i Dīnī nazd-i Ahl-i Sunnat," *Shish Guftār dar bārih-yi Dīn va Jāmi'a*, Tehran 1352 AHS/1974.

Ḥasan Ḥanafī, "al-Tafsīr wa Maṣāliḥ al-Umma: al-Tafsīr al-Ijtimāʿī, *Qaḍāyā' Islāmiyya Muʿāṣara*, no. 4 (1419/1998).

Ḥasan Ḥanafī, *al-Turāth wa al-Tajdīd Mawqifunā min al-Turāth al-Qadīm*, Beirut 1412/1992.

Ḥasan ibn ʿAbd Allah ʿAskarī, *Muʿjam al-Furūq al-Lughawiyya, al-Ḥāwī li-Kitāb Abī Hilāl al-ʿAskarī wa Juzʾan min Kitāb al-Sayyid Nūr al-Dīn al-Jazāʾirī*, Qum 1412/1992.

Ḥasan ibn Muḥammad Naẓẓām al-Aʿraj, *Tafsīr Gharāʾib al-Qurʾan wa Raghāʾib al-Furqān*, Zakariyā ʿUmayrāt, ed., Beirut 1416/1996.

Ḥasan Ṣadr, *Taʾsīs al-Shīʿa li-ʿUlūm al-Islām*, [Baghdad 1370/1950] Tehran offset reprint [n.d.].

Ḥaydar ibn ʿAlī Āmulī, *Jāmiʿ al-Asrār wa Manbaʿ al-Anwār*, Henri Corbin, ʿUthmān Ismāʿīl Yaḥyā, eds., Tehran 1368 AHS/1989.

Ḥaydar ibn ʿAlī Āmulī, *Tafsīr al-Muḥīṭ al-Aʿẓam wa al-Baḥr al-Khiḍamm fī Taʾwīl Kitāb Allah al-ʿAzīz al-Muḥkam*, Muḥsin Mūsawī Tabrīzī, ed., Tehran 1416/1995.

Hidāyat Jalīlī, *Rawish-shināsī-yi Tafāsīr-i Mawḍūʿī-yi Qurʾan*, Tehran 1372 AHS/1993.

Ḥimayda Nayfar, *al-Insān wa al-Qurʾan Wajhan li-Wajh*, Dār al-Bayḍāʾ (Casablanca) 1997.

Hudā Jāsim Muḥamamd Abū Ṭabara, *al-Manhaj al-Atharī fī Tafsīr al-Qurʾan al-Karīm: Ḥaqīqatuhū wa Maṣādiruhū was Taṭbīqātuhū*, Qum 1414/1994.

Ḥusayn ibn Masʿūd Baghawī, *Tafsīr al-Baghawī al-Musammā Maʿālim al-Tanzīl*, Khālid ʿAbd al-Raḥmān al-ʿAkk and Marwān Sawār, Beirut 1415/1995, Tehran offset reprint 1363 AHS/1984.

Ḥusayn ibn Muḥammad Rāghib Iṣfahānī, *al-Mufradāt fī Gharīb al-Qurʾan*, Muḥammad Sayyid Kaylānī, Tehran [1332 AHS/1953?].

Ḥusayn ibn Muḥammad Rāghib Iṣfahānī, *Muqaddima Jāmiʿ al-Tafāsīr maʿa Tafsīr al-Fātiḥa wa Maṭāliʿ al-Baqara*, Aḥmad Ḥasan Farḥāt, ed., Kuwait 1405/1984.

Ibn Abī al-Ḥadīd, *Sharḥ Nahj al-Balāgha*, Muḥammad Abū al-Faḍl Ibrāhīm, ed., Cairo 1385-1387/1965-1967, Beirut offset reprint [n.d.].

Ibn Anbārī, *al-Bayān fī Gharīb I'rāb al-Qur'an*, Ṭāhā 'Abd al-Ḥamīd Ṭāhā, Egypt [n.d.], Qum offset reprint 1362 AHS/1983.

Ibn 'Arabī Muḥammad ibn 'Abd Allah, *Qānūn al-Ta'wīl*, Muḥammad Sulaymānī, ed., Beirut 1990.

Ibn 'Arabī Muḥammad ibn 'Alī, *al-Futūḥāt al-Makiyya*, Dār al-Ṣādir, Beirut [n.d.].

Ibn 'Aṭiyya, *al-Muḥarar al-Wajīz fī Tafsīr al-Kitāb al-'Azīz*, vol. 1, [Rabat] 1395/1975.

Ibn 'Aṭiyya, *al-Muḥarar al-Wajīz fī Tafsīr al-Kitāb al-'Azīz*, vol. 1, Raḥḥālī Fārūq et al, eds., Doha 1398/1977.

Ibn 'Aṭiyya, *Muqaddimatān fī 'Ulūm al-Qur'an*, Arthur Jeffrey, 'Abd Allah Ismā'īl Ṣāwī, eds., Cairo 1392/1972.

Ibn 'Asākir, *Ta'rīkh Madīna Dimashq*, 'Alī Shīrī, ed., Beirut 1415-1421/1995-2000.

Ibn 'Āshūr, *Tafsīr al-Taḥrīr wa al-Tanwīr*, Tunis 1984.

Ibn Bābiwayh, *Ma'ānī al-Akhbār*, 'Alī Akbar Ghaffārī, [Qum] 1361 AHS/1982.

Ibn Bābiwayh, *Thawāb al-A'māl wa 'Iqāb A'māl*, Najaf 1972, Qum offset reprint 1364 AHS/1985.

Ibn Bābiwayh, *'Uyūn Akhbār al-Riḍā*, Ḥusayn A'lamī, ed., Beirut 1404/1984.

Ibn Durayd, *Kitāb al-Jamhara al-Lugha*, Ramzī Munīr Ba'labakī, ed., Beirut 1987-1988.

Ibn Fāris, *Mu'jam Maqāyyīs al-Lugha*, 'Abd al-Salām Muḥammad Hārūn, ed., Qum 1404/1984.

Ibn Ḥajar 'Asqalānī, *Fatḥ al-Bārī: Sharḥ Ṣaḥīḥ al-Bukhārī*, Dār al-Ma'rifa, Beirut [n.d.].

Ibn Ḥajar 'Asqalānī, *Kitāb al-Iṣāba fī Tamyyīzx al-Ṣaḥāba*, Egypt 1328/1910, Beirut offset reprint [n.d.].

Ibn Ḥanbal, *Musnad Aḥmad ibn Ḥanbal*, Istanbul 1402/1982.

Ibn Hishām, *Mughnī al-Labīb 'an Kutub al-A'ārīb*, Muḥammad Muḥy al-Dīn 'Abd al-Ḥamīd, ed., Cairo [n.d.].

Ibn Jawzī, *Zād al-Masīr fī 'Ilm al-Tafsīr*, Beirut 1404/1984.

Ibn Jinnī, *al-Khaṣā'iṣ*, Muḥammad 'Alī Najjār, ed., [Cairo 1372-1376/1952-1957], Beirut offset reprint [n.d.].

Ibn Jinnī, *al-Muḥtasib fī Tabyyīn Wujūh Shawādh al-Qirā'āt wa al-Īḍāḥ 'anhā*, Muḥammad 'Abd al-Qādir 'Aṭā, Beirut 1419/1998.

Ibn Jizzī, *Kitāb al-Tashīl li-'Ulūm al-Tanzīl*, Beirut 1403/1983.

Ibn Kathīr, *al-Bidāya wa al-Nihāya*, 'Alī Shīrī, ed., Beirut 1408/1987.

Ibn Kathīr, *Tafsīr al-Qur'an al-'Aẓīm*, 'Alī Shīrī, ed., Beirut [n.d.].

Ibn Kathīr, *Tafsīr al-Qur'an al-'Aẓīm*, Beirut 1412/1991.

Ibn Khāliwayh, *I'rāb al-Qirā'āt al-Sab' wa 'Ilaluhā*, 'Abd al-Raḥmān ibn Sulaymān 'Uthaymīn, Cairo 1413/1992.

Ibn Khāliwayh, *I'rāb Thalāthīn Sūra min al-Qur'an al-Karīm*, Beirut 1411/1991.

Ibn Manẓūr, *Lisān al-'Arab*, Dār al-Ṣādir, 15 vols., Beirut 1955.

Ibn Nadīm, *al-Fihrist*, Riḍā Tajaddud, ed., Asadī, Tehran 1350 AHS/1971.

Ibn Qutayba, *Ta'wīl Mushkil al-Qur'an*, Aḥmad Ṣaqr, ed., Cairo 1393/1973.

Ibn Qutayba, *Tafsīr Gharīb al-Qur'an*, Aḥmad Ṣaqr, Cairo 1378/1958.

Ibn Rashīq, *al-'Umda fī Maḥāsin al-Shī'r wa Ādābuhū wa Naqduhū*, Muḥammad Muḥy al-Dīn 'Abd al-Ḥamīd, ed., Beirut 1401/1981.

Ibn Sa'd, *Tabaqāt al-Kabīr*, Eduard Sachau, ed., 8 vols., E.J.Brill, Leiden 1904-19401, Iḥsān 'Abbās, ed., Beirut 1957-1968.

Ibn Ṣalāḥ, *Fatāwā wa Masā'il Ibn Ṣalāḥ fī al-Tafsīr wa al-Ḥadīth wa al-Uṣūl wa al-Fiqh*, 'Abd al-Mu'ṭī Amīn Qal'ajī, ed., Beirut 1406/1986.

Ibn Ṣalāḥ, *Muqaddima Ibn Ṣalāḥ wa Maḥasin al-Iṣṭilāḥ*, 'Ā'isha 'Abd al-Raḥmān Bint al-Shāṭi', ed., Cairo 1974.

Ibn Shū'ba, *Tuḥaf al-'Uqūl 'an Āl al-Rasūl*, 'Alī Akbar Ghaffārī, Qum 1363 AHS/1984.

Ibn Ṭāwūs, *Sa'd al-Su'ūd li-'l-Nufūs*, Fāris Tabrīziyān Ḥassūn, ed., Qum 1379 AHS/2000.

Ibn Taymiyya, *Muqaddima fī Uṣūl al-Tafsīr*, Dār al-Maktaba al-Ḥayāh, Beirut [n.d.].

Ibn Taymiyya, *al-Tafsīr al-Kabīr*, 'Abd al-Raḥmān 'Umayra, ed., Beirut 1408/1988.

Ibrāhīm 'Aṭwa 'Iwaḍ, *Min al-Ṭabarī ila Sayyid Quṭb: Dirāsāt fī Manāhij al-Tafsīr wa Madhāhibihi*, Cairo 1421/2000.

Ibrāhīm ibn Mūsā Shāṭibī, *al-Muwāfaqāt fī Uṣūl al-Aḥkām*, [Cairo 1341/1992], offset reprint [Cairo, n.d.].

Ibrāhīm ibn Mūsā Shāṭibī, *al-Muwāfaqāt fī Uṣūl al-Sharī'a*, Muḥammad 'Abd Allah Dirāz, ed., Beirut 1395/1975.

Ibrāhīm ibn Sirrī Zajjāj, *I'rāb al-Qur'an*, Ibrāhīm Abyārī, ed., Beirut 1406/1986.

Ibrāhīm ibn Sirrī Zajjāj, *Ma'ānī al-Qur'an wa I'rābuhū*, 'Abd al-Jalīl 'Abduh Shalabī, ed., Beirut 1408/1988.

Ignaz Goldziher, *Madhāhib al-Tafsīr al-Islāmī*, 'Abd al-Ḥalīm Najjār, tr., Cairo 1374/1955.

'Iliyyīn Ibrāhīm Qumī, *Tafsīr al-Qumī*, Ṭayyib Mūsawī Jazā'irī, ed., Qum 1404/1983.

'Iliyyīn Yūsuf Qifṭī, *Ta'rīkh al-Ḥukamā' wa huwa Mukhtaṣar al-Zūzanī al-Musammā bi-'al-Muntakhabāt al-Multaqaṭāt min Kitāb Ikhbār al-'Ulamā' bi-Akhbār al-Ḥukamā'*, Lippert, ed., Leipzig 1903.

Ilyās Kalāntarī, *Dalīl al-Mīzān fī Tafsīr al-Qur'an*, Tehran 1362 AHS/1997.

Ismā'īl ibn Ḥammād Jawharī, *al-Ṣiḥāḥ: Tāj al-Lugha wa Ṣiḥāḥ al-'Arabiyya*, Aḥmad 'Abd al-Ghaffūr 'Aṭṭār, ed., Beirut [n.d.], Tehran offset reprint 1368/1989.

Ismāʿīl ibn Muḥammad Mustamlī, *Sharḥ al-Taʿarruf li-Madhhab al-Taṣawwuf*, Muḥammad Rawshan, ed., Tehran 1363-1366 AHS/1984-1987.

Ismāʿīl ibn Muṣṭafā Ḥaqqī, *Tafsīr Rūḥ al-Bayān*, Beirut 1405/1985.

Ismāʿīl Pāshā Baghdādī, *Īḍāḥ al-Maknūn fī al-Dhayl ʿalā Kashf al-Ẓunūn*, Istanbul 1971-1972.

Jaʿfar Shahīdī, "Tafsīr, Tafsīr bi-Raʾy, Tārīkh wa Ḥudūd Istifādih az Ān," in *Farkhundih Payām: Yādigār-nāmih-yi Ustād Duktur Ghulāmḥusayn Yūsufī*, Mashhad University, Mashhad 1360 AHS/1981.

Jalāl al-Dīn Muḥammad ibn Muḥammad Mawlawī, *Mathnawī-yi Maʿnawī*, Reynold Allen Nicholson, Naṣr Allah Pūrjavādī, eds., Tehran 1363 AHS/1984.

Johann Fück, *Taʾrīkh Ḥaraka al-Istishrāq: al-Dirāsāt al-ʿArabiyya wa al-Islāmiyya fī Urūbā ḥattā Bidāya al-Qarn al-ʿIshrīn*, translated from German by ʿUmar Luṭfī ʿĀlim, Beirut 2001.

Junayd ibn Maḥmūd Shīrāzī, *Shadd al-Izār fī Ḥaṭṭ al-Awzār ʿan Zawwār al-Mazār*, Muḥammad Qazvīnī, ʿAbbās Iqbāl Āshtiyānī, eds., Tehran 1328 AHS/1949, Tehran reprint 1366 AHS/1987.

Kāẓim Bargniysī, "Vāzhih-hāyi Dakhīl-i Qurʾan va Didgāh-hā," *Maʿārif*, vol. 12, nos. 1-2 (Farvardīn-Ābān 1374 AHS/March-November 1995.

Khalīl ibn Aḥmad Farāhīdī, *Kitāb al-ʿAyn*, Mahdī Makhzūmī, Ibrāhim Sāmarrāʾī, eds., Qum 1405/1984.

Khaṭīb Baghdādī, *al-Kifāya fī ʿIlm al-Riwāya*, Ḥaydarābād Dakkan 1315/1897.

Khaṭīb Baghdādī, *Taʾrīkh Baghdād*, 14 vols., Maṭba al-Saʿāda, Cairo 1307-1310/1889-1892.

Māhir Mahdī Hilāl, *Fakhr al-Dīn Rāzī Balāghiyyan*, Baghdad 1397/1977.

Maḥmūd ibn ‘Abd Allah Ālūsī, *Rūḥ al-Ma‘ānī*, Dār al-Iḥyā’ al-Turāth al-‘Arabī [n.d.].

Maḥmūd ibn ‘Abd al-Karīm Shabistarī, *Gulshan-i Rāz*, Aḥmad Mujāhid, Muḥsin Kiyānī, eds., Tehran 1371 AHS/1992.

Maḥmūd Rāmyār, *Tārīkh-i Qur’an*, Tehran 1362 AHS/1983.

Maḥmūd Ṭāliqānī, *Partuwī az Qur’an*, vol. 1, Tehran 1345 AHS/1966.

Makkī ibn Abī Ṭālib Ḥammūsh, *Mushkil I‘rāb al-Qur’an*, Ḥātam Ṣāliḥ Ḍāmin, ed., Beirut 1407/1987.

Ma‘mar ibn Muthannā Abū ‘Ubayda, *Majāz al-Qur’an*, Muḥammad Fu’ād Sizgīn, ed., Cairo 1988.

Manī‘ ‘Abd al-Ḥalīm Maḥmūd, *Manāhij al-Mufassirīn*, Cairo 1421/2000.

Mas‘ūd ibn ‘Umar Taftāzānī, [*Sharḥ*] *al-‘Aqā’id al-Nasafiyya*, Istanbul 1326/1908, Baghdad offset reprint [n.d.].

Mas‘ūdī, *Murūj al-Dhahab*, 7 vol., Beirut 1966-1974.

Muḥammad ‘Abd al-‘Aẓīm Zarqānī, *Manāhil al-‘Irfān fī ‘Ulūm al-Qur’an*, Cairo [1980].

Muḥammad ‘Abduh, *al-A‘māl al-Kāmila li-Imām Muḥammad ‘Abduh*, Muḥammad ‘Ammāra, vol. 5: *Fī Tafsīr al-Qur’an*, Beirut 1973.

Muḥammad ‘Abduh, *Risāla al-Tawḥīd*, Beirut 1396/1976.

Muḥammad Aḥmad Khalaf Allah, *al-Fann al-Qiṣaṣī fī al-Qur’an al-Karīm*, edited and annotated by Khalīl ‘Abd al-Karīm, Beirut 1999.

Muḥammad A‘lā ibn ‘Alī Tahānawī, *Kitāb Kashshāf Iṣṭilāhāt al-Funūn*, Muḥammad Wajīh et al, eds., Culcutta 1862, Tehran offset reprint 1967.

Muḥammad A‘lā ibn ‘Alī Tahānawī, *Mawsū‘a Kashshāf Iṣṭilāḥāt al-Funūn wa al-‘Ulūm*, Rafīq al-‘Ajam, ‘Alī Daḥrūj, Beirut 1996.

Muḥammad ‘Alī Ayāzī, “Nigāhī bih Tafāsīr-i Mawḍū‘ī-yi Mu‘āṣir,” *Kayhān Andīshih*, n. 28 (Bahman-Isfand 1368 AHS/1989.

Muḥammad Bāqir Ḥakīm, *‘Ulūm al-Qur’an*, Tehran 1403/1982.

Muḥammad Hādī Ma'rifat, *al-Tafsīr wa al-Mufassirūn fī Thawba al-Qashīb*, Mashhad 1418-1419/1997-1998.

Muḥammad Ḥusayn 'Alī Ṣaghīr, *al-Mabādī al-'Āmma li-Tafsīr al-Qur'an al-Karīm bayn al-Naẓariyya wa al-Taṭbīq*, Beirut 1420/2000.

Muḥammad Ḥusayn Dhahabī, *al-Tafsīr wa al-Mufassirūn*, Beirut 1407/1987.

Muḥammad Ḥusayn Ṭabāṭabā'ī, *al-Mīzān fī Tafsīr al-Qur'an*, Dār al-Kutub al-Islāmiyya, Tehran 1361-1362 AHS/1982-1983.

Muḥammad ibn 'Abd Allah Ḥākim Nayshābūrī, *Kitāb Ma'rifa 'Ulūm al-Ḥadīth*, Sayyid Mu'aẓẓam Ḥusayn, ed., Ḥaydarābād Dakkan, 1937, Medina offset reprint 1397/1977.

Muḥammad ibn 'Abd Allah Ḥākim Nayshābūrī, *al-Mustadrak 'ala al-Ṣaḥīḥayn*, Yūsuf 'Abd al-Raḥmān Mar'ashlī, Beirut 1406/1985.

Muḥammad ibn 'Abd Allah Iskāfī, *al-Mi'yār wa al-Muwāzana fī Faḍā'il Amīr al-Mu'minīn 'Alī ibn Abī Ṭālib (AS)*, Muḥammad Bāqir Maḥmūdī, ed., Beirut 1402/1981.

Muḥammad ibn Aḥmad Dhahabī, *Tadhkira al-Ḥuffāẓ*, Ḥaydarābād Dakkan 1956-1958, Beirut offset reprint [n.d.].

Muḥammad ibn Aḥmad Qurṭubī, *al-Jāmi' li-Aḥkām al-Qur'an*, Dār al-Fikr, Beirut [n.d.].

Muḥammad ibn Aḥmad Qurṭubī, *al-Jāmi' li-Aḥkām al-Qur'an*, vol. 1, pt. 1, Cairo 1387/1967, vol. 2, pt. 3, Beirut [1376/1957?], vol. 7, pt. 13, Cairo 1387/1967, Tehran offset reprint 1364 AHS/1985.

Muḥammad ibn 'Alī Dāwūdī, *Ṭabaqāt al-Mufassirīn*, Beirut 1403/1983'

Muḥammad ibn 'Alī Ḥakīm Tirmidhī, *Taḥṣīl Naẓā'ir al-Qur'an*, Ḥusnā Naṣr Zaydān, [Cairo] 1389/1969.

Muḥammad ibn 'Alī Shawkānī, *Fatḥ al-Ghadīr*, Dār al-Iḥyā' al-Turāth al-'Arabī, Beirut [n.d.].

Muḥammad ibn 'Azīz Sijistānī, *Gharīb al-Qur'an al-Musammā bi-Nuzha al-Qulūb*, Beirut 1402/1982.

Muḥammad ibn Bahādur Zarkashī, *al-Burhān fī 'Ulūm al-Qur'an*, Yūsuf 'Abd al-Raḥmān Mar'ashlī, Jamāl Ḥamdī Dhahabī, Ibrāhīm 'Abd Allah Kurdī, eds., Beirut 1410/1990.

Muḥammad ibn Ḥasan affār Qumī, *Baṣā'ir al-Darajāt fī Faḍā'il Āl Muḥammad (SAW)*, Tehran 1362 AHS/1983.

Muḥammad ibn Ḥasan Raḍī al-Dīn Istarābādī, *Sharḥ Shafiyya Ibn al-Ḥājib*, Muḥammad Nūr al-Ḥasan, Muḥammad Zafzāf, Muḥammad Muḥy al-Dīn 'Abd al-Ḥamīd, Beirut 1395/1975, Tehran offset reprint [n.d.].

Muḥammad ibn Ḥusayn Sharīf Raḍī, *Talkhīṣ al-Bayān fī Majāzāt al-Qur'an*, Muḥammad 'Abd al-Ghanī Ḥasan, ed., Beirut 1406/1986.

Muḥammad ibn Ḥusayn Sulamī, *Majmū'a-yi Āthār-i Abū 'Abd al-Raḥmān Sulamī: Bakhsh-hā'ī az Ḥaqā'iq al-Tafsīr wa Rasā'il-i Dīgar*, Naṣr Allah Pūrjavādī, ed., Tehran 1369-1372 AHS/1990-1993.

Muḥammad ibn Ibrāhīm Ṣadr al-Dīn Shīrāzī, *Mafātīḥ al-Ghayb*, annotated by 'Alī Nūrī, edited by Muḥammad Khʷājawī, Tehran 1363 AHS/1984.

Muḥammad ibn 'Īsā Tirmidhī, *al-Jāmi' al-Kabīr*, Bashshār 'Awwād Ma'rūf, ed., [Beirut] 1998.

Muḥammad ibn Luṭfī Ṣabbāgh, *Buḥūth fī Uṣūl al-Tafsīr*, Beirut 1408/1988.

Muḥmmad ibn Mas'ūd 'Ayyāshī, *Kitāb al-Tafsīr*, Hāshim Rasūlī Maḥallātī, ed., Qum 1380-1381/1960-1961, Tehran offset reprint [n.d.].

Muḥammad ibn Mas'ūd 'Ayyāshī, *al-Tafsīr*, Qum 1421/2000.

Muḥammad ibn Muḥammad Abū al-Su'ūd, *Tafsīr Abī al-Su'ūd al-Musammā Irshād al-'Aql al-Salīm ila Mazāyā al-Qur'an al-Karīm*, Dār al-Iḥyā' al-Thurāth al-'Arabī, Beirut [n.d.].

Muḥammad ibn Muḥammad Ghazālī, *Iḥyā' 'Ulūm al-Dīn*, Beirut 1412/1992.

Muḥammad ibn Muḥammad Ghazālī, *Mishkāt al-Anwār wa Miṣfāh al-Asrār*, 'Abd al-'Azīz 'Izz al-Dīn Sayrawān, ed., Beirut 1407/1986.

Muḥammad ibn Muḥammad Māturīdī, *Tafsīr al-Māturīdī al-Musammā Ta'wīlāt Ahl al-Sunna*, Ibrāhīm 'Iwaḍayn, Sayyid 'Iwaḍayn, eds., Cairo 1391/1971.

Muḥammad ibn Muḥammad Murtaḍā Zabīdī, *Tāj al-'Arūs min Jawāhir al-Qāmūs*, 'Alī Shīrī, ed., Beirut 1414/1994.

Muḥammad ibn Muḥammad Riḍā Qumī Mashhadī, *Tafsīr Kanz al-Daqā'iq wa Baḥr al-Gharā'ib*, Ḥusayn Dargāhī, ed., Tehran 1366 [-1370] AHS/1987-[1991].

Muḥammad ibn Shāh Murtaḍā Fayḍ Kāshānī, *Tafsīr al-Ṣāfī*, Ḥusayn A'lamī, ed., Beirut [1399/1979?].

Muḥammad ibn Sulaymān Kāfiyajī, *Kitāb al-Taysīr fī Qawā'id 'Ilm al-Tafsīr*, Ismā'īl Jarrāḥughlī, ed., Ankara 1974.

Muḥammad ibn 'Umar Fakhr Rāzī, *al-Tafsīr al-Kabīr*, Cairo [n.d.], Tehran offset reprint [n.d.].

Muḥammad ibn Ya'qūb Fīrūzābādī, *Baṣā'ir Dhawi al-Tamyyīz fī Laṭā'if al-Kitāb al-'Azīz*, vols. 1-2, Muḥammad 'Alī Najjār, ed., Beirut [n.d.].

Muḥammad ibn Ya'qūb Fīrūzābādī, *Tartīb Qāmūs al-Muḥīṭ*, Ṭāhir Aḥmad Zāwī, ed., Beirut 1399/1979.

Muḥammad ibn Ya'qūb Kulaynī, *Uṣūl al-Kāfī*, Dār al-Ta'āruf li-'l-Maṭbū'āt, Beirut 1411/1990.

Muḥammad ibn Yazīd Mubarrad, *al-Kāmil*, Ibrāhīm Dalmajūnī Azharī, ed., Cairo 1339/1920.

Muḥammad ibn Yazīd Mubarrad, *al-Muqtaḍab*, Muḥammad 'Abd al-Khāliq 'Uḍayma, ed., Beirut [1382/1963].

Muḥammad Muḥsin Āqā Buzurg Ṭihrānī, *al-Dharī'a ila Taṣānīf al-Shī'a*, Mu'assissa-yi Ismā'īliyān, Qum 1355 AHS/1977.

Muḥammad Pāshā Makhzūmī, *Khāṭirāt Jamāl al-Dīn al-Afghānī al-Ḥusaynī*, Beirut 1931.

Muḥammad Rashīd Riḍā, *Tafsīr al-Qur'an al-Ḥakīm al-Shahīr bi-Tafsīr al-Manār*, vol. 1, notes taken at the teaching sessions held by Shaykh Muḥammad 'Abduh, Egypt 1373/1953.

Muḥammad Riḍā Shafī'ī Kadkanī, "Chihrih-yi Dīgar-i Muḥammad ibn Karrām Sijistānī dar Partaw-i Sukhanān-i Nu-yāftih az Ū," in: *Arj-nāmih-yi Īraj: bih Pās-i Nīm Qarn Savābiq-i Darakhshān-i Farhangī va Dānishgāhī Ustād*

Īraj Afshār, Muḥsin Bāqirzādih, ed., vol. 2, Tūs, Tehran 1418-1419/1997-1998.

Muḥammad Taqī Subḥanī, "Qur'an wa Sarchishmih-hāyi Taṣawwuf az Didgāh-i Khāvarshināsān-i Mu'āṣir: Nigāhī Intiqādī bih Kitāb-i Tafsīr va Zabān-i 'Irfānī [by] Paul Noya," *Bayyināt*, vol. 2, no. 3 (Autumn 1374 AHS/1995).

al-Muqaddimāt min Kitāb Naṣṣ al-Nuṣūṣ fī Sharḥ Fuṣūṣ al-Ḥikam li-Muḥy al-Dīn Ibn al-'Arabī, vol. 1, Henri Corbin, Ismā'īl Yaḥyā, eds. Tehran 1353 AHS/1975.

Muqātil ibn Sulaymān, *Tafsīr Muqātil ibn Sulaymān*, 'Abd Allah Maḥmūd Shaḥḥāta, [Cairo] 1979-1989.

Murtaḍā 'Askarī, *al-Qur'an al-Karīm wa Riwāyāt al-Madrasatayn*, Tehran 1373-1376 AHS/1994-1997.

Murtaḍā Karīmīniyā, "Kitābshināsī-yi Muṭāli'āt-i Tafsīrī dar Zabān-hāyi Urūpā'ī," *Faṣlnāmih-yi Pazhuhish-hāyi Qur'anī*, vol. 7, nos. 25-26 (spring-summer 1380/2001.

Musā'id ibn Sulaymān Ṭayyār, *Fuṣūl fī Uṣūl al-Tafsīr*, Riyadh 1420/1999.

Muṣṭafā ibn 'Abd Allah Ḥājī Khalīfa, *Kashf al-Ẓunūn 'an Asāmī al-Kutub wa al-Funūn*, 7 vols., Dār al-Kutub al-'Ilmiyya, Beirut 2008.

Muṣṭafā Muslim, *Mabāḥith fī al-Tafsīr al-Mawḍū'ī*, Damascus 1421/2000.

Muṣṭafā Ṣāwī Juwaynī, *Manāhij fī al-Tafsīr*, Mansha' al-Ma'ārif, Iskandariyya [n.d.].

Muwaffaq ibn Aḥmad Akhṭab Kh^wārazm, *al-Manāqib*, Mālik Maḥmūdī, ed., Qum 1417/1996.

Najīb 'Aqīqī, *al-Mustashriqūn*, Cairo 1980-1981.

Paul Noya, *Tafsīr-i Qur'anī va Zabān-i 'Irfānī*, Ismā'īl Sa'ādat, tr., Tehran 1373 AHS/1994.

Ruzbahān-nāmih, Muḥammad Taqī Dānishpazhūh, ed., Anjuman-i Āthār-i Millī, Tehran 1347 AHS/1968.

Ṣāḥib ibn 'Abbād, *al-Muḥīṭ fī al-Lugha*, Muḥammad Ḥasan Āl Yāsīn, Beirut 1414/1994.

Sa'īd Shartūnī, *Aqrab al-Mawārid fī Fuṣuḥ al-'Arabiyya wa al-Shawārid*, Qum 1403/1982.

Ṣalāḥ Ṣāwī, "Rūzbahān va Tafsīr-i 'Arā'is al-Bayān," *Taḥqīqāt-i Islāmī*, vol. 1, no. 2-vol. 2, no. 1 (1365-1366 AHS/1986-1987.

Sayyid Quṭb, *Fī Ẓalāl al-Qur'an*, Beirut 1386/1976.

Ṣiddīq Ḥasan Khān, *Fatḥ al-Bayān fī Maqāṣid al-Qur'an*, Beirut 1420/1999.

Shawqī Ḍayf, *al-Balāgha: Taṭawwur wa Ta'rīkh*, Cairo [1965?].

Shukrī Muḥammad 'Iyād, *Yawm al-Dīn wa al-Ḥisāb*, [n.p.] 1980.

Ṣubḥī Ṣāliḥ, *Dirāsāt fī Fiqh al-Lugha*, Beirut 2000.

Ṣubḥī Ṣāliḥ, *Mabāḥith fī 'Ulūm al-Qur'an*, Beirut 1968, Qum offset reprint 1363 AHS/1984.

Sulaymān Ātash, *Maktab Tafsīr Ishārī*, Tawfīq H. Subḥānī, tr., Tehran 1381 AHS/2002.

Sulaymān ibn Ash'ath Abū Dāwūd, *Sunan Abī Da'ūd*, Muḥammad Muḥy al-Dīn 'Abd al-Ḥamīd [Cairo, n.d.], [Beirut] offset reprint [n.d.].

'Ulūm al-Qur'an 'ind al-Mufassirīn, Markaz al-Thaqāfa wa al-Ma'ārif al-Qur'aniyya, Qum 1374-1375 AHS/1995.

'Umar Riḍā Kaḥḥāla, *al-'Ulūm al-Dīn al-Islāmī*, Damascus, 1394/1974.

Yaḥyā ibn Ḥamza Yamanī, *Kitāb al-Ṭirāz al-Mutaḍḍamin li-Asrār al-Balāgha wa ʿUlūm Ḥaqāʾiq al-Iʿjāz*, Beirut 1402/1982.

Yaḥyā ibn Ziyād Farrā', *Maʿānī al-Qurʾan*, vol. 1, Aḥmad Yūsuf Najātī, Muḥammad ʿAlī Najjār, eds., Egypt 1955, Tehran offset reprint [n.d.].

Yaḥā ibn Sharaf Nawawī, *al-Taqrīb wa al-Taysīr li-Maʿrifa Sunan al-Bashīr wa al-Nadhīr*, Muḥamamd ʿUthmān Khisht, Beirut 1405/1985.

Yūsuf ibn Abī Bakr Sakkākī, *Miftāḥ al-ʿUlūm*, Cairo 1356/1937.

Zayd ibn ʿAlī (AS), *Tafsīr Ghaīb al-Qurʾan*, Muḥammad Jawād Ḥusaynī Jalālī, ed., Qum 1376 AHS/1997.

INDEX